the world's your Lobster

Also by Joe Bennett

Just Walking the Dogs (Hazard Press)
Sleeping Dogs and Other Lies (Hazard Press)
Fun Run and Other Oxymorons (Scribner UK)
So Help Me Dog (Hazard Press)
Sit (Hazard Press)
Bedside Lovers (and Other Goats) (Scribner UK)
Doggone (Hazard Press)
Barking (Hazard Press)
A Land of Two Halves (Simon & Schuster UK)
Unmuzzled (Hazard Press)
Dogmatic (Hazard Press)
Mustn't Grumble (Simon & Schuster UK)
Down Boy (Hazard Press)
Eyes Right (And They's Wrong) (HarperCollins)
Where Underpants Come From (Simon & Schuster UK)
Life, Death, Washing-up, etc. (Simon & Schuster UK)
Alive and Kicking (HarperCollins)
Laugh? I Could Have Cried (HarperCollins)

the World's your Lobster

JOE BENNETT

HarperCollinsPublishers

The columns that make up this collection first appeared in the *Press*, the *Dominion Post*, the *Otago Daily Times*, the *Southland Times*, the *Waikato Daily Times*, *Hawke's Bay Today*, the *Northern Advocate* and *New Zealand Gardener*.

National Library of New Zealand Cataloguing-in-Publication Data
Bennett, Joe, 1957–
The world's your lobster / Joe Bennett.
ISBN 978-1-86950-810-4
1. New Zealand wit and humor—21st century. 2. New Zealand—
Social life and customs—21st century—Anecdotes. I. Title.
NZ828.202—dc 22

First published 2009
HarperCollins*Publishers (New Zealand) Limited*
PO Box 1, Shortland Street, Auckland 1140

Copyright © Joe Bennett 2009

Joe Bennett asserts the moral right to be identified as the author of this work.

All rights reserved. No part of this publication may be reproduced, stored in a retrieval system or transmitted in any form or by any means, electronic, mechanical, photocopying, recording or otherwise, without the prior written permission of the publishers.

ISBN 978 1 86950 810 4

Cover design by Sarah Bull
Cover image by Photosouth Photographers
Typesetting by Janine Brougham

Printed by Griffin Press, Australia

70gsm Classic used by HarperCollins*Publishers* is a natural, recyclable product made from wood grown in sustainable forests. The manufacturing processes conform to the environmental regulations in the country of origin, Finland.

For Nemo

contents

Yours sincerely 9
Bwana Pope 13
Proust for one 17
Classifieds 20
A small thing but mine own 25
Know this, America 29
Round the block 32
Free as a bird 35
The hole in the pocket 38
Look away now 42
From Solon to this 45
Gee 20 49
Tape ends 52
Lessons of the land 56
Here's Y 60
Up Lab Coat Ave 63
Encouraging and true 67
How I did good 70
Showdown mit Gott 73
The Beast 76
On the buses 80
IYP to IYR 83

O Holy Co 86

Thanks, mole 89

Playing nice 92

Experts say 95

Coming to get you 98

Lovefruit 102

Naomi's good 105

On buying a jogger 108

The reality is 111

Nuts 115

Bye-bye, little nothing 118

Investigating booze 121

Meant for someone else 124

By any other name 127

Recalling the grizzly 130

Whale problems 133

The liturgy remains 136

Water works 141

Tip it in 144

Go away and leave me alone 147

Ida down 151

The day before Christmas 154

Yours sincerely

Dear Mr B. Racer,

Greetings. I hope this finds you upset.

In pursuance of Infraction Order 1571 and in accordance with the requirements of the Fair Warning Act (2009) I am writing to inform you that the vehicle registered in your name, to wit a Nissan Fartah, registration number BTTLPGS, together with all appurtenances attached thereunto and modifications made thereunto, including, though not necessarily consisting entirely of, a lowered suspension system, a musical reproduction device with the capacity to deafen at a range of 30 metres a cow or similar domesticated animal (as specified in the Emergency Powers Act 2009, subsection Specious Bovine Audiology Test), seats of the variety known as 'bucket' and a muffler that converts engine noise into a sound resembling that of a pre-World War II machine gun (manufacturer unspecified) will be, at dawn on the morning of the Fifth Day of February in the Year of Our Lord Two Thousand and Nine at the place known as Tyburn Hill, crushed.

It is anticipated that the abovementioned vehicle will be reduced from an estimated volume of 7 cubic metres to an approximate volume of 1 cubic metre. The registration of the vehicle, indeed the existence of the vehicle as a vehicle per se, will thereinafter legally cease. (I am obliged to inform you that the precise point in the procedure at which the vehicle ceases to be a vehicle has yet to be defined in a court of law. Should you wish to test this point, academic though it may be since the moment the crusher makes its first impression on your property it becomes effectively beyond repair, and certainly beyond the capacity of your wallet to repair, given the fines that will be raining down on you as God's displeasure rained down on Sodom, I feel it incumbent on me to warn you that the denizens of Her Majesty's bench, being of middle age or greater and of a sedentary suburban habit, are generally representative of the citizenry whom you have spent the last 18 months of your brief and ignorant life enraging, and are, frankly, unlikely to look with favour on any pedantic legal quibbling emanating from a defendant such as yourself, or, more likely, given your educational record, from some legal counsel hired by your indulgent parents, guardians, caregivers or any combination thereof. In short, and I trust you will forgive the informality, don't try it, sonny.)

You will be pleased to learn that the unexpired portion of your vehicle registration will be refunded to you by the relevant authority. You may be less pleased to learn, perhaps, that the full and unrelieved cost of the towing, impoundment and destruction of your vehicle, along with all associated costs such as my time, which I can assure you I am spinning out in order to inflict the maximum possible financial pain on you while taking the greatest care to remain within the guidelines of permissible bureaucratic expenditure, will, by order of the court, be borne by the vehicle owner, i.e. you. And it is as sure as eggs are reproductive devices that the costs will exceed the reimbursement by a factor of at least 50.

By natural justice, the crushed vehicle remains your property. In consequence any hire purchase arrangements made with a finance company or similar entity, or their receivers and debt recovery officers (who are frequently former military men who will visit you in a manner not entirely unreminiscent of the manner in which you visited quiet suburban streets in your soon-to-be-former vehicle) remain in force. Furthermore you will be required to make arrangements for the disposal of the crushed remains of your vehicle, and in the event of any unreasonable delay in effecting such arrangements, you will be charged rental for the space occupied by the said remains. The rates for this rental have been set by a decree, the wisdom of which I can only applaud, at a level likely to exceed even the hourly rate charged by the bewigged whore of a lawyer that your parents, guardians, caregivers or combination thereof may have hired to defend you.

Finally I would like to extend a cordial and indeed heartfelt invitation to you to attend the crushing ceremony. But I would advise you to arrive early. These events are proving hugely popular with the middle classes. Unable to afford more commercial pleasures in these straitened times, they have taken to attending crushings in numbers exceeding those attending rugby union test matches. The atmosphere is of a festival nature.

And should you choose to attend you will be made acquainted with sentiments whose vengeful ferocity of expression will remind you, should you be capable of such introspection, of precisely the same sort of bestial ranting that you were once accustomed to spend your Friday and Saturday evenings bellowing at the sky and at any unfortunate citizens or police officers who happened to cross your benighted path.

Please accept my insincere expression of sympathy at your sad loss.

Her Majesty's Officer of Crushing.

Bwana Pope

When the last pope keeled over I was worried. And when they announced that an elderly German would be taking over the lease on the Popemobile, I came close to the sin of despair. I've nothing against Germans, but few have been known for their charisma. Even when I heard that the new papa had the promising nickname of 'God's Rottweiler', I still didn't hold out much hope.

Well, I couldn't have been more wrong. Old Ratzinger's proved a cracker. He kicked off by saying nasty things about Islam. Then when World Youth Day was held in Sydney, he not only flew down there himself and paraded through the streets in a Perspex cage, but he also sent the remains of a dead saint in a box with which to wow the youngsters.

Being a stickler for tradition, he's maintained the habit of protecting priests who've been naughty with choirboys. He's reinstated a bishop who thinks that the holocaust wasn't really as bad as all that. And now he's popped down to Africa to tell the locals how to behave. You've got to love him.

Here's a transcript of a recent meeting between him and the ordinary people of Africa.

Ordinary People of Africa: Welcome, your Holiness, to our great continent which, despite being the probable origin of the human species, has had a pretty tough time of it in the last few hundred years, what with slavery, colonial exploitation, rapacious missionaries, home-grown dictators, vicious civil wars, and an invasion of people in shorts making nature documentaries for the fat telly addicts of the west.

Pope: Thank you.

Ordinary People of Africa: Not to mention assorted celebrities winging down here to demonstrate their concern for us by hugging a few orphans. Sometimes they even take an orphan home with them as a souvenir, though we don't mind that too much because . . .

Pope: I think that's enough moaning.

Ordinary People of Africa: Sorry. But the good news is that over 20 million of us are infected with HIV or Aids, which is roughly two-thirds of the world's cases, so there's a ready supply of orphans to keep your celebrities happy.

Pope: No condoms.

Ordinary People of Africa: What?

Pope: You heard me. Condoms only make things worse. The way to prevent the spread of Aids is to abstain from sex until you marry someone who has also abstained from sex and then never to have sex with anyone else. So said God.

Ordinary People of Africa: When and where?

Pope: A long time ago in the Bible.

Ordinary People of Africa: Where in the Bible exactly?

Pope: What lovely weather you have in Africa.

Ordinary People of Africa: Thank you, your Holiness. You are very kind. But are you really suggesting that we Africans should behave in a way that no human society has ever behaved or ever will behave, and that if we don't, which we won't, we must just die, when all the time there's a simple, cheap and proven device for preventing the disease, a device that the Bible says nothing about because it didn't exist when the Bible was written?

Pope: Yes.

Ordinary People of Africa: Do you perhaps subconsciously see Aids as God's vengeance on the wicked? No offence, your Holiness, we just want to know where we stand.

Pope: Isn't it pretty the way the sun catches the headstones in that cemetery? Oh, I nearly forgot, no witchcraft either.

Ordinary People of Africa: What?

Pope: You heard me. This witchcraft stuff has got to stop. Stop listening to supposedly holy men with big juju. They are just frauds and charlatans who invoke imaginary spiritual powers in order to wring money from people who can't afford it. All that religious mumbo-jumbo of theirs, the elaborate rituals, prayers for this, incense for that, exist only to dupe the gullible. Ditto all that fancy finery they wear. Crikey, it's hot here in Africa.

Ordinary People of Africa: Oh, you poor white thing. Let us relieve you of some of your fancy finery, or perhaps that incense swinger with which you like to waft smoke over us while intoning stuff in a language none of us understands.

Pope: Thank you. That's better. The trouble with witchcraft, you see, is not just that it's superstitious nonsense that does no good, but also that it puts unelected people in positions of unwarranted power. As a result these shamsters get to make pronouncements that directly affect the lives and deaths of people who didn't appoint them. It's got to stop, do you hear me? Oh, and I bet lots of those witch doctor chaps take sexual advantage of their dupes. Am I right?

Ordinary People of Africa: Is the Pope a Catholic?

Proust for one

Ah, birthdays. So very Proustian, don't you think? A chance, as it were, to stand still.

Three hundred and sixty-four days a year we trudge through the sandstorm of petty events, battered, blown and insignificant, our eyes screwed to slits (though nails do the job just as well), our teeth gritted (mine by now are little more than stubs), keeping on keeping on, head down, our vision limited to the yard or so of tawny humdrum necessity at our feet. No time to look up. No time to be.

But then, whoa, the one day of the year, the day of birth, the day that marks us as special, a day, Lord bless it, when we alone matter (along with the occasional other chap with whom by some extraordinary quirk of fate we happen to share that day, those few numbering only 1/365th (and a quarter) of the population of the globe which, if you discount the beasts of the field, as most people do, though I am uncertain why, especially when you consider dogs, is 6.5 billion, more or less, meaning that we share our day of unique self-importance with only 17,808,219 cherished brothers and sisters, dogs not included, each of whom, the cherished brothers and sisters, that is, we would be delighted to meet in order to oooh at the freakishness of coincidence. Though personally I'd rather meet the dogs.)

And when annually that special day dawns, as reliable as my dog's disobedience, it is the chance to raise the head and ask, Where am I? Because a birthday invites us to take stock, to perform a little tour d'horizon (Oh, why do the French do such phrases so very well? Is it the wine do you think, or the halitosis?) to note the passage of another year and to reflect on the state of life's little journey, to consider where we are going and whether we have got any closer, or whether indeed there is anything to get closer to, and whether, if we did manage to get close to it, we would actually like the look of it, whatever it might be, or whether perhaps the notion of destination is a delusion, and that the destination is actually the journey itself, if, that is, the journey itself isn't a delusion. For who is to say that we are not as donkeys on a waterwheel, endlessly moving but returning always to old ground? Don't you think so? Don't you feel that?

For today, as you may perhaps have guessed, is my birthday and I am performing right now my tour d'horizon, or rather I would be performing it were it not for an endless stream of phone calls from well-wishers and friends and other intimates of that uniquely affectionate region of the anatomy, my bosom. Both of them (the well-wishers and friends, that is, rather than the bosom, which, in defiance of appearance, is generally considered singular) began the phone call with a resounding 'Happy birthday'.

Oh, the tone of it. So jovial. Yet for all the friends and well-wishers knew, I could have been at that moment undergoing prep for a quintuple amputation, or I could have just been diagnosed with terminal what do you call it, you know, where you keep forgetting the names of things. But 'Happy birthday', they said, for that is the formula.

And they said it so cheerfully when they had no cause to be cheerful. It was not, after all, their birthday. They were still battling the daily sandstorm, eyes screwed, teeth etc.

So was their bonhomie fake? Were they merely being nice to me, in the wish that I would be happy? Or were they perhaps feeling pleased with themselves at the thought of their own generosity and loyalty for having not only remembered my birthday but also for having done something about it, though not, in either case, I couldn't help noticing, to the extent of instructing a courier to deliver a crate of something chilled to my home address with which they are both familiar, having each knocked back far more than a crate themselves within its welcoming walls.

So was the congratulation that they flung at me flung really at themselves for having demonstrated themselves to be good chaps? A curmudgeonly thought, I admit, but a thought that did flit like a black moth across my tour d'horizon until I swatted it.

'Thank you,' I said, playing my part as per script. 'Thank you so much. You are very kind.'

At which point in both conversations we arrived at a hiatus (an hiatus? I am unsure. I find that on birthdays I am unsure of much.) They had spoken. I had spoken. There seemed, momentarily, nothing else to say.

To plug the hiatus they asked whether I had anything planned for my big day. I said I planned to write a column about birthdays, explaining how they were so very Proustian.

'Ah yes,' they said. And then they talked about themselves. I am 52.

Classifieds

FOR SALE

For sale: As is where is. Child in full working order. Chocolate brown. May be African. Would suit aging international pop star with much money and no integrity. Can be orphaned if necessary. (Other models and colours may be available.)

For sale: Interactive battery-operated Australian NRL player doll. Add alcohol, set loose on town, then arrest. Educational. Handcuffs extra.

For sale: Pilates. Free postage on orders of a dozen or more. No known uses but delivered in sturdy attractive box. Gift-wrapping service available.

Free to good home: Joggers. Found abandoned on beach in weighted sack. Ugly but endearing. Not house trained. In urgent need of neutering. Email number required and preferred sex to SPCJ@Self-Lothian.com. (NB Females can bite.)

LOST AND FOUND

Lost: Adolescent good looks, somewhere between Swiss bank and American football pitch. Of no value to finder. To owner, sole means of support. Reward offered. Send to D. Beckham, Edge of Precipice Villa, Approaching Middle Age, Oh My God, Los Angeles.

Lost: Presumed stolen. Priceless art installation. New Zealand's entry at Venice Biennale. Comprises symbolically unplugged electronic devices the arrangement of which explores aspects of 21st-century alienation and commercial consumption within a bicultural context. Described by *Listener* art critic as 'evocative and eerily resonant'.

Found: Eyebrows. Discovered wandering near loch. Had to be subdued. If unclaimed will be euthanased and used as pot scourers.

Found: Heap of junk. Mostly defunct electronic devices. Free to anyone willing to take it away. Contact Venice Municipal Waste Disposal Authority.

Lost: Election, control over everything, and any desire to remain in country to which unswerving devotion has been sworn. If found send by international gravy train to H. Clark, c/o UNHCR, Acronym City.

Lost in vicinity of Wall Street: Several trillion dollars. Presumed evaporated. Reward offered of shares in Lehman Bros.

Found: Small skulking thing. Possibly a homoeopath. Would make good pet for caring family.

Lost: Framed diploma (summa cum laude) from the Centre for Digital Autoproctology. Great sentimental value. Return to Unelected, Oblivionstrasse, Tauranga. Reward offered of an audience with the owner.

Lost: Eyebrows. One pair. Distinctive. Much missed. Stolen under anaesthetic during involuntary plastic surgery at PR Styling Agency. May have shreds of integrity attached. No need to post. Just tell them firmly to go home to Overnight Singing Sensation, Spinsterville, Scotland.

Lost: Empire. Deeply loved and never forgotten. Last seen all over the world about 100 years ago. Send by registered mail to The Occupant, Several Palaces, UK. (Postage free. Addressee owns the mail service.)

Lost: In the vicinity of late middle age everywhere. A bag embroidered with the word 'Yesterday'. Contains summers of endless sunshine, community solidarity, defined roles for the sexes, family values, real entertainment, unlocked doors, unquestioning happiness, a sense of permanence and chocolate bars three times the size they are today. If found do not subject to close scrutiny.

Found: Responsible teenage motorist. Possibly unique. Expressions of interest invited from research institutes, museums and vivisectors.

Found: Gullibility. For further information send $5.

Found in mid-Canterbury by the entire South Island police force, the Armed Offenders Squad and several helicopters. Nobody.

Lost: Innocence.

WANTED

Wanted for immediate destruction. Lycra. All of it. Post to Society for Aesthetic Action in the Interest of Public Well-being.

Wanted: By kleptomaniac.

SITUATIONS VACANT

Position available for figurehead. Duties include incoherent bluster, and riding single-seater political vehicle designed in form of throne. Coherent political philosophy irrelevant. Absence of principles essential. Send CV to New Zealand First, the Wilderness.

Telephone survey takers required. Must be available to work at mealtimes.

BIRTHS, MARRIAGES AND DEATHS

To Greed and Hubris of New York. One Financial Crisis.

PERSONALS

Prof m, 61, n/s, gsoh, seeks am f. 16, s, nsoh.

Narcissist seeks similar.

Nihilist seeks

Thanks to St Jude, patron saint of lost causes, for resurrection of the word pandemic and the rising panic over swine flu. From a grateful virologist who predicted the end of the world through bird flu.

ADULT ENTERTAINMENT

Massage: For the sports fanatic. Blonde Suzanna does sports specials: linseed oil and wicketkeeping gloves; sensual rucking, etc. Snooker a speciality. No croquet.

For sale: Novel by Justin Cartwright. Dissects and delineates with unflinching precision the unease of the human beast and the societies he forms. Way over the heads of children. Entertainment for adults at its very best. (*Sure this is in the right section? Ed.*)

TRADE

For trade on Trade Me. Me. Will exchange for nicer model or an ounce of civet.

A small thing but mine own

A dishevelled elderly man appeared in the district court this morning charged with abusing a police officer in a manner likely to cause a breach of the peace. Holding his head in bandaged hands and groaning, the defendant accepted a glass of water from the usher but refused an aspirin, saying that he stood for truth and there was no way he was going to be bought off.

A police constable told the court that at two o'clock the previous morning he had discovered the defendant in Cathedral Square beating with bloodied fists on the doors of *The Press*. He was in an emotional condition and calling for 'a sub-editor or sub-editors unknown' to emerge and 'put up your dukes'. The defendant gave his name as Britney Spears. When asked whether he had a home to go to, the defendant became abusive.

Judge: Come, come, now, officer. Tell us what he said. We don't flinch from a little ripe language in this court.

Officer: Very well, your honour. The defendant told me to 'piddle off'. Whereupon he burst into maniacal laughter, fell to the ground and writhed there, clutching his belly. Much as he is doing right now in the dock.

Judge: The defendant is warned that contempt carries a penalty of 30 days' custodial.

Defendant: (Rising with some difficulty to his feet) I will stand. But I can't stand much more of this. (Dry laughter from defendant only.)

Officer: At the police station a credit card receipt was found in his pocket issued by an outlet licensed to purvey spirituous liquors. It revealed that the defendant was in fact a J. Bennett of Lyttelton, apparently a writer.

Judge: A writer, eh? Well, let's see if he can write his way out of this one. (Sycophantic laughter from the *Press* court reporter, who alone occupied the public benches.) Was any explanation of his behaviour forthcoming?

Officer: He maintained repeatedly and at a volume that kept the station awake for much of the night that he had been the victim of intolerable provocation in the form of sub-editing 'most foul and treacherous'. It seems that he writes a column for the said publication and it had been edited in a manner that sat ill with him.

Judge: I see. Well now, Mr Bennett, what have you got to say for yourself?

Defendant: If you have tears, your honour, prepare to weep them now.

Judge: I shall not warn you about contempt a third time, Mr Bennett.

Defendant: If it please your honour, in my weekly article, a small thing but mine own, I made use of a word, a word of four letters, to wit a p, the third vowel and a brace of s's. It is an ancient word, of lineage stout and pedigree unbesmirched. It is to be found in the King James Bible. It is to be found in Chaucer. Should your honour wish me to quote from *The Wife of Bath's Tale* written circa 1390, a text on the curriculum of every university literature course in the English-speaking world, he has only to say so.

Judge: I am a busy man, Mr Bennett.

Defendant: Yet before the article was published some footling, style-guide-driven functionary, some worm, saw fit to replace my sturdy monosyllable with the bisyllabic horror of piddle. I ask you, your honour, piddle. At a stroke he had shifted the tone from a forthright masculinity to a prissy infantilism. Piddle, your honour, belongs in the playground. It is of a piece with wee-wee. Or Number Twos. Or spending an asterisking penny.

I care not what you do to me, your honour. Whip me, scourge me, clap me in irons. I stand for truth, as better people have stood before me, in the Star Chamber, at the Inquisition, at the Chatterley trial, and I am proud to stand beside them. What have we come to that we should fear four little letters in print?

Judge: Did you or did you not tell the constable to piddle off?

Defendant: Mea ipsissima verba.

Judge: I'll have no French spoken in this court.

Defendant: I spoke those words, your honour.

Judge: And the word piddle is one that *The Press*, that longstanding organ of respectability, is content to publish?

Defendant: Sadly so, your honour.

Judge: Then there is no abuse and no case to answer. The defendant, I regret to say, is free to leave. Though I advise him off the record and man to man to stay off the piddle.

The sycophantic giggle of the court reporter was drowned by a roar as the defendant was swept from the courtroom by his own two adoring feet and carried similarly through the streets where he strewed flowers in his own path and he cheered himself hoarse wherever he went and bestowed upon himself the name of Implacable Foe of Censorship and other mighty titles before taking refuge from the acclamation in a pub.

Know this, America

Know this, America. We have nothing to fear but getting carried away with sonorous oratory.

For yea, verily, I say unto you who are watching this inauguration on televisions in the little village where my father was born, or on rather larger and more expensive televisions in the ornate clubhouse of a golf course in Dubai where the waiters are drawn from the poor countries of the world and the patrons from the rich ones, the waiters being dark of skin and slim of frame while the patrons are white of skin and generally speaking fat, I am come.

And what I bring unto you in my coming is my youth, my coffee-coloured skin, my transparent decency, my calm, my confidence, or at least the expression of my confidence, and my heritage of high-flown biblical diction.

And so it comes to pass that I have inherited an empire in decline, an empire with a shrinking GDP and a maxed-out credit card and bankers lobbing themselves from the windowsills of Manhattan, and you look to me to lead you through the Valley of the Shadow of Death and across the Desert of Thorns and up the rugged Mountains of Difficulty until we shall behold from the summit the promised land of stable house prices and a thriving automotive industry, a promised land that looks remarkably similar to the one we inhabited only a year or two ago. People, I hear you.

I feel your yearning to be released from unwise and

unwinnable wars against an indefinable enemy. I share your desire to return to pre-eminence among the peoples of the world and to have once again more money than anyone else and to be able to go on foreign holidays and photograph poor people being decorative without having to fear being bombed.

   I am but one frail man. Cut me and I bleed. But I accept the mantle that you have thrust upon my shoulders, and I accept the crown that you have placed upon my head, and I do hereby vow to roll up my sleeves, mindful though I am that mantles generally do not come with sleeves, and go to work. And I ask of you only, my fellow Americans, that you too roll up your sleeves and go to work with me, though how you actually set about doing this if you've just lost your job, I shall let pass for the moment, for this is an inaugural speech and is therefore long on sonorous metaphor but short on specifics.

   'E pluribus unum', my friends, out of many shall come one. Out of many candidates for the presidency has come one president. And out of that one president have come many allusions, allusions to John F. Kennedy, to Martin L. King and to The H. Bible. And out of the many words that have been spoken about this president, and the many votes that have been cast for him, and the many, many dollars that have been flung at him, has come one clear and present danger. That danger is an emotional condition that has begun to sweep the globe, from the plains of Africa where my father was born, to the golf clubs of Dubai where he wasn't, but where, incidentally, I am amused to learn, there was a raucous cheer as my no-good predecessor climbed aboard a chopper and disappeared from public view for good and ever. I am aware that right now in this speech I am exploiting that emotional condition just a teensy weensy bit because it is a potent force, but I am also aware of its absurdity and its danger. It is an emotional condition that the human beast has always been susceptible to and it has probably done more harm and killed more people and enslaved more people than any other. I am afraid, my friends, that you have begun to see me as the messiah.

For though the parallel is inexplicit and I shall make damn sure I keep it that way, it is most certainly implicit and active. I come from outsider stock. I rose from nothing to the throne. I bring a message of hope and revival. I have vowed to scourge the greedy and to succour the poor in spirit. I shall uplift the little errand boy and I shall spank the bankers. I bring hope of a new way and a new dawn. I am come unto you in your hour of need when the ice caps are melting and the Chinese have got our money and the bailiffs are at the door and the realtors weep and the recreational vehicles stand forlorn and unwanted on the sales yard and the ghouls cackle at our backs, and I bring tidings of great joy. Beware, my friends and fellow Americans. Beware belief. Belief can move mountains. But it tends to put them back down in the wrong place.

Round the block

Adults sometimes ask me a question. I don't know why. I try never to ask questions myself. Assert, is my motto, and then assert again more loudly. My family crest features a bald man in earplugs with a megaphone rampant. At his feet a carpet of unquestioning dogs.

For that's the nice thing about dogs. Because they are rightly convinced that their little parcel of instincts is quite enough to get them through the world, they don't ask questions. In this they are much like the adolescents I used to teach, except that the adolescents could have done with asking a few questions. Such as 'Can I really expect someone to employ me when I dress like a mendicant, slouch like Quasimodo and grunt like a Wimbledon ladies' champion?' or 'Do I really believe that wealth, ease and the latest game-playing technology will drop into my lap from the summer sky without my ever having to raise a finger or exude a drop of sweat?'

But before we look at the question adults ask, let's look at the word adult. It has two definitions. One is grown-up, responsible, mature, wielding one's local body election vote in an informed and selfless manner. The other definition of adult is sexually explicit. The two definitions appear to be at odds. One implies that adults have transcended the adolescent preoccupation with sex. The other implies that they haven't. And if you take an evening stroll along Patpong

Road you will rapidly discover which is the true one, at least for blokes. The adult male is just an adolescent who has learnt to dissemble. Time has encrusted him with a shell that is halfway presentable and has taught him hypocrisy. That's it.

But anyway, a remarkable number of adults ask me a question. They ask me whether I suffer from . . . well, what infirmity do you think they name?

Halitosis? Wrong. You don't have to ask whether someone suffers from halitosis. And anyway, the halitotic don't suffer. It's the people they talk to that suffer.

For some reason halitosis is endemic among schoolteachers. A disproportionate number of the men and women who taught me or taught with me had breath that could wither a geranium at 20 paces. Perhaps it is the body's instinctive defence against adolescents.

So people don't ask me about halitosis. They ask me whether I suffer from writer's block. Or rather Writer's Block.

Once I've recovered the power of speech I ask a question.

I know, I know, I denied asking questions. But this is a Trojan question, a question that is leading to an assertion as inevitably as wealth leads to decadence. 'What do you do?' I ask.

My interlocutor gapes like a goldfish. He or she is unaccustomed to having sniper fire returned.

'Come on,' I say, 'what do you do?'

'Bricklaying,' they say, 'or investment banking, or I farm scallops.'

'I see,' I say gravely, cradling my chin between thumb and forefinger in the manner of a photographer's subject who wishes to appear thoughtful. 'So tell me, do you ever suffer from Bricklayer's Block, or Banker's Block? Do you ever get up in the morning, behold your scallop boat lying tilted on the strand and go into a funk of incapacity, screaming, "No, no, I simply can't, don't expect it of me, it's just too much for a sensitive soul to cope with, oh help me, ye gods, take pity on this poor mortal whose juices have suddenly run dry"?'

'Well no,' they say. Then after a pause comes a chuckle and, 'but there are a few mornings when . . .'

'Precisely,' I scream, 'and on those few mornings, when you simply don't want to lay bricks or bank or dredge scallops, when it all seems too much, what do you do?'

'Knuckle down,' they say, 'just grin and go to it. The misery passes. But bricklaying or banking or scalloping isn't like writing, is it? It isn't, you know, creative.'

At this point I am tempted by anger. 'Creative' makes my intestines curdle. And I've got plans for it. I'm going to take it round the back of the abattoir and waterboard it in the best American manner, waterboard it till it squeals for mercy.

Creative means making stuff, and everyone makes stuff. Bricklayers make walls, bankers make deals and scallop fishermen make raids on the sea. None of these things would exist did not the people create them. But somehow the word creative has been hijacked by the quiveringly indolent and the self-obsessed and applied only to the arts. The result is that incompetent daubs and transcultural installations count as creative whereas the infinitely better built and more admirable gallery that shelters them from the cruel indignity of actual weather belongs somehow to a lower order of making.

To which I say, 'Hah'. Assertively. No more questions.

Free as a bird

Six months ago, as alert readers may recall, I built what I thought was a chicken coop. But it's now turned out to be a metaphor.

I made the thing for free with scraps from my garage. A friend who found me at work on it asked if it was an art installation. I said of course, and I was thinking of entering it for the Venice Biennale.

'You mean?' he said.

'Precisely,' I said. 'Inherent in this superficially ramshackle structure is a fusion of cultural motifs. Here is the myth of rural improvisation on which this country's Pakeha identity is built, interwoven with references to traditional Maori structural forms. Thus this ambiguous piece explores our national sense of self, suggesting both harmony and dislocation. Simultaneously spiritual and pragmatic, it is a work both for and of our times.'

'Sounds like a shoo-in for Venice,' he said.

'It's a chicken coop,' I said.

'Oh,' he said. Then he pointed. 'What's to stop the chooks escaping through there?'

'This bit of wood,' I said and I nailed it home.

Having finished the coop I used cunning and a handful of wheat to trap three chooks in it, and once they'd recovered their equilibrium they set to work laying eggs.

Oh, those eggs. To compare a fresh, almost free-range

egg with a supermarket egg is to compare a Vermeer with anything at the Venice Biennale. These eggs were as rich as Bernie Madoff used to be. When you cracked them into a pan, they stood as tall as they lay wide. I feasted all summer long and the dog even got a few.

But I felt guilty. Apparently the only four words that Hitler knew in French were 'Vous êtes mon prisonnier'. And the chooks were mine. I had taken from them the one thing that makes life worthwhile, which is not beer, nor love, nor art installations, nor yet *Dancing with the Stars*, but autonomy.

My guilt made me treat the captives like guests at the best hotel. I fed them on corn and feed pellets and sumptuous leftovers, and I shifted the coop onto fresh grass each day, and I gave them the softest hay to nest in, and I taught the dog not to terrify them. But whenever their non-captive sisters came to cluck at them through the mesh, I felt a pang. The other birds were free as birds. These three were gaolbirds.

Yet I did not release them. My greed for eggs overrode the mutterings of conscience. And with the help of whatever shiraz was on $5.99 special at Woolworths, I managed to sleep of nights.

Then autumn spread its russet mantle over the land. And as my prose turned purple, egg production fell. It fell like a Wall Street graph and came to rest on the y-axis. The chooks were spent. They would not lay again till spring came dancing over the hilltops like Julie Andrews with a gaggle of von Trapps.

So I let the birds go. The breeze of freedom would play once more through their feathers. They would be chooks again, wandering the world as whim dictated, unfettered, unhampered, unanythinged, just birds as birds were meant to be under the good wide skies of chance. And as I propped open the door of their prison, I felt, to use an avian metaphor, that an albatross had fallen from my wrinkled neck, or perhaps, to use a non-avian metaphor, as a penitent must feel when he kneels in the confessional.

I poured a shiraz, summoned the dog, said, 'Come, my friend, let us drink to autonomy' and I chinked the glass against his collar. Then together we sat to watch the chooks rediscover the world.

We sat for an hour. One of the chooks peeped out through the open door, then withdrew. Dusk fell. I took the dog for a walk, then the bottle to bed. In the bright morning I went out to inspect. The door was still propped open and the chooks were still inside. They stayed there all day. And I fell to thinking.

'O dog,' I said that evening, 'do you not see what this means? It says everything, not about chooks, but about the human condition. That we prefer the chains of incarceration to the random winds of chance. That we choose to be the prisoners of habit. It is habit that enables us to bear the long journey of our days. The boon of liberty is too terrifying a boon. That thing there, my friend, is no hen coop. It's a stonking great metaphor.'

The chooks left prison the next morning.

The hole in the pocket

So you want to get into high finance. Good on you. Here's a four-step guide.

Step 1 — find a hobo. He should be homeless, hopeless and with a hole in his pocket through which money tumbles straight to the liquor store.

Offer him a loan. The loan is to let him buy a modest house in which he can entertain friends to methylated cocktails round the heated swimming pool. But don't forget to put an inflated valuation on the house first.

When the hobo accepts, assume the role of mortgage broker. In other words, sell the loan to someone else. It may seem like a bad loan to you, but lending institutions will jump at it. Add a cut for yourself, and hey presto, you've started making money. But there's a lot more cash to be made further up the ladder.

Step 2 — become a lender. As a lending institution, you must always remember that one bad debt is a bad thing, but a lot of bad debt is a good thing. So buy as many hobo-loans as you can. Sweep them up like confetti after a wedding.

You'll soon have loans by the fistful. A few will be sound but most will be lousy. Just bundle them together and slice the bundle into sellable units, each of which has a bit of each loan in it. The process is simple, but you must make it seem complicated so that commentators will refer to it as sophisticated financial engineering. Everyone's impressed by sophisticated financial engineering, especially when you give it an impenetrable name like collateralised debt obligations. To obfuscate matters even more you can then reduce this to CDO. Initials lend status. And anyone who doesn't understand them is reluctant to admit their ignorance.

Now sell your CDOs to venerable financial institutions such as investment banks. They'll snap them up and you'll have made a nice fat profit. Once again you can stop there, but step three beckons the brave.

Step 3 — become boss of an investment bank that buys CDOs. This has the immediate advantage of paying a hilarious salary. But it comes with a hitch. Remember the hobo? Having held a couple of poolside parties, he felt the call of the open road and simply walked off the property. But he did remember to drop the keys in an envelope. So you now have the keys to a house that is worth less than the loan you advanced on it. This is known in financial circles as negative equity and in less financial circles as a problem.

But in the world of high finance every problem is an opportunity in disguise. Just file for bankruptcy. Almost immediately the US cavalry will arrive in the form of the US Treasury. They'll buy your bad loans and you'll get a fat golden handshake that is more than enough to retire on. But you may find you've enjoyed the ride so much that you want to go on to step 4.

Step 4 — become President of the United States of America, a position that comes with enormous prestige. But it also comes with a trillion dollars' worth of CDOs, which have now been stripped of their verbal finery and have reverted to what they always were which is plain bad loans. You've bought them in the name of the people who originally took them out. And you've used their taxes to pay for them. So effectively the American people now own a trillion dollars' worth of bad loans to themselves. And most of the money has just plain disappeared. House prices have shrunk and the rest of the cash has gone to China in exchange for goods that the American people are too sophisticated to make for themselves.

To prop up the American people you need money fast. But your only reliable source of money is taxes levied on the American people, and in order to achieve the presidency you promised to lower taxes on the American people rather than raise them. To compound your problems you're running a colossal trade deficit and you've got some expensive wars to fight in the name of the American people. So your only choice is to borrow from the people who've now got the money that used to be American. So off you trot to Beijing, selling Treasury bonds. These are effectively mortgages on the United States.

Then all you have to do is to cross your fingers and hope that the Chinese don't ask for their money back before your term in office ends. You really don't want to be the first US president to take step 5.

Step 5 — pop the keys to your country into an envelope and take to the open road, homeless, hopeless and with a hole in your pocket through which money tumbles straight to the liquor store.

Good luck in your financial careers.

Look away now

Like psychics, astrologers and the bearded ladies of the Treasury, I make predictions. Unlike them I get things right.

Three weeks ago, even before the first TV announcer had thrown the first cheap sneer at China, I gave you the Olympic results in full. I announced that Valerie Vili would win gold, that China would win the ping pong and that the continent of Africa would win no prizes for swimming. All bang right.

I further predicted that most of the swimming medals would go to the fattest nation on earth. Imagine my delight, then, when Michael Phelps won another race and the camera scanned the crowd. One spectator had a stars and stripes flag and a belly like a hammock full of blancmange. In the excitement he leaped from his seat to the extent that he was capable of leaping. Inertia held his belly where it was. But as he came down again his belly rose. Momentarily we lost sight of his face.

I got some things wrong. I correctly predicted the skin colour of the 100-metre winner but not that he would be 3 metres tall. Nor did I predict that he would run only 75 metres. At that point he was so far ahead he stopped sprinting and for the rest of the race he just skipped like a spring lamb. And he still broke the world record. In the best Olympic tradition it was pure freak show.

I also failed to predict the Hungarian weightlifter's elbow. 'Look away now,' said the TV frontman when they showed the clip. Like everyone else I did the exact opposite: I leaned forward on the sofa in expectation of schadenfreudist delight.

Success in weightlifting is obvious. The lifter goes from looking like a dog shitting to looking like a starfish stretching. The starfish posture defines triumph. Every quivering hair in the starfish's armpit bellows *yes*.

The Hungarian was trying to lift 145 kilos, which is about five well-fed Labradors. He squatted, grunted then heaved. Veins bulged. He came within millimetres of success. Then his elbow popped.

The verb popped doesn't quite convey the drastic nature of what happened. His elbow bent the wrong way. The change in the man's demeanour was remarkable.

Unsurprisingly, but unwisely, he let go of the bar. All five Labradors landed on his neck. It was as if gravity was giving him an extra smack for his hubris. Here was the hollow cruelty of ambition that Macbeth discovered. For four years this man had dreamed of lifting more weight above his head than any other man of a similar size in the world. Now he dreamed of returning to what he had been throughout those four years, which was a man with an elbow that worked.

As he fell forward in agony he had the presence of mind to fling out his ruined arm so that it lay in full view of the camera. Then he went into spasm as if Tasered. For you and me on the sofa of indolence, it was like having a front-row seat at a car crash.

Then, and almost as wonderfully, half a dozen minions

shuffled on. They were carrying screens which they posed between the camera and the victim. The only time I've seen anything similar was at a race meeting in England. A horse fell at a fence and broke its leg. Rather less promptly than in Beijing, men surrounded the horse with screens. Then they shot it. I don't think they shot the Hungarian.

I was surprised that the screens weren't decorated with ads for the official Olympic credit card. But I was even more surprised that no commentators took the chance to have another dig at China. Here was the ideal metaphor.

In China, they could have said, yet again, you only get to see what they want you to see. It's been a constant snide refrain since the opening ceremony when the little girl lip-synched and some of the images of fireworks were computer-generated. Oh, what deceptive and manipulative buggers they are.

Well now, I don't deny for one minute that China is keen to create a good impression. Nor do I deny for one minute that the Chinese authorities are imperfect. But what I do question is the right we have to condemn them. We in the west, whose prosperity is founded on commercial delusions that stretch from here to my Aunt Fanny; we in the west who uncritically swallow the staged banalities of politics and television; we in the west with our PR companies and our communications directors and our spin doctors; and we in the west who've accepted an invitation to China to enjoy a global freak show. At best our criticism is ignorant, smug and rude. At worst it's mere hypocrisy. And predictable hypocrisy at that.

From Solon to this

A dishevelled elderly man appeared in the Christchurch District Court this morning charged with smoking tobacco in a public park.

'I've seen that face in this court before, I believe,' said the judge, peering over his glasses. The defendant made no response, being preoccupied with rummaging through the pockets of his overcoat.

Judge: Am I right?

Defendant: There's a first time for everything, your honour.

Judge: Ah yes, now it's coming back to me: the impertinence, the intemperance, that overcoat, and that disdain for the law, the nobility of which stands between the race of men and the quagmire of barbarism. Your name will come to me in a minute. Bandit, wasn't it, or something similar?

Defendant: Your honour is perhaps confusing me with a legal acquaintance.

Judge: Bennett, that was it. Some sort of writer chap.

Defendant: Your honour is a marvel of retention.

Judge: That's enough of your lip, do I make myself clear?

Defendant: As a bull sea elephant on the foggy shores of Punta Arenas.

Judge: And I'll have none of your far-fetched and supercilious metaphors, thank you.

Defendant: It was a simile, your honour.

Judge: And very simile, if I may say, to contempt of court.

This remark was greeted with sycophantic laughter from the court reporter, for which the judge asked that his gratitude be recorded in the transcript of proceedings.

The Crown asserted that in the early hours of that morning a Smoking Enforcement Officer had been conducting a routine patrol of Hagley Park golf course when his attention was drawn to a glow emanating from bushes near the 16th tee.

Defendant: Is a man not allowed to light his path home any more? Is this a fit nation for free men?

'Silence,' boomed the judge.

Defendant: I don't suppose you've got an aspirin on you? I've got a head like a steam hammer.

The judge warned the defendant that contempt carried a penalty of 30 days' custodial.

Crown: When the officer called out, the defendant emerged from the bush in an unsteady fashion and asked whether the officer had 'a wee drop of the good stuff to wash down an old soldier's last gasper'. In addition to the smoke from the defendant's cigarette, the officer noted a strong smell of spirituous liquor. When informed that he was being arrested for smoking tobacco in a public place, the defendant gave his name as 'the immortal Oscar'.

Judge: Wilde, I presume.

Crown: Indeed he was, your honour. He flailed his arms and shouted abuse in such an extravagant manner that the officer felt obliged to call for back-up. The arrest was eventually effected by a Swift Response Unit from the Council Anti-Smoking Helicopter Squadron. The defendant had to be subdued with a Taser.

Defendant: Three shots they fired, and me an old man. The first two got my hip flask. Not the first time that hip flask has done me service, I can tell you. Why, I remember when your honour would have been no more than a babe in arms, and I was off serving Queen and country in the jungles of Malaya, up to my neck in leeches and forfeiting my youth to preserve a decent world for your honour to grow up into with every advantage, and this flask, the very same one I tell you, stopped . . .

Judge: Your record makes no mention of military service.

Defendant: It was metaphorical, your honour.

Judge: You are despicable.

Defendant: A metaphor expressive of decline, your honour, decline from Solon's great vision of a just democracy, to a world where the authorities enact a law against smoking that fails to observe the fundamental moral and legal distinction between a crime that harms others and a vice that harms only the perpetrator. And what justifications do they offer for this monstrous legal wrong? One, that the sight of a broken old man having a consolatory gasper in public might cause innocent children to take up the habit (those same innocent children whom they consider immune to the influence of a billion explicit murders on television). And two, that the rest of the world is enacting similar legislation and so they'd better follow suit. Only dead fish swim with the stream, your honour. Solon and I say nuts to them and nuts again. Clap me in gaol. I don't care.

Judge: What? Throw you into a prison cell that by some legal quirk is deemed a private residence where a man may smoke as he wishes? No, I sentence you to continue to inhabit free society, to come to terms with change, to stop whining and to grow up.

Resisting vigorously as he was led away to freedom, the defendant announced his intention to appeal.

Gee 20

Now can you see why I didn't attend the G20 in London? Gosh, it was grisly.

Needless too. The whole thing could have been done in cyberspace. Even the most callow and zit-laden of Bill Gates' underlings could have built the great leaders a virtual conference centre had they truly wished to have a serious and inexpensive chat. But they didn't wish. They insisted on lugging their flesh to London.

Why? Well, the point about elected leaders is that they have always wanted to be elected leaders. So every one of them has dedicated the last 20 years or so to getting elected. They've said what's expedient. They've greased the mob. They've cosied up to money. They've led sanitised private lives. They've talked on talk shows. They've been lobbied and advised and told what message to purvey. In the process they've watched their autonomy dissolve like a Kleenex in the rain. And they've learnt to play a role. They've become, of necessity, actors. And actors exist only when on stage. The G20 was a chance to strut.

Barack took along a bomb-proof Cadillac, his wife, 500 goons and advisers, and a squadron of decoy helicopters with which to bamboozle any Abdul al Grudge who might be lurking in the wilds of Essex with a rusting missile launcher.

But what the goons and choppers couldn't thwart was that

buffoon Berlusconi with his oiled head and the face like a Halloween pumpkin. Every time Barack smiled for the camera up popped the media Mussolini behind him, making rabbit ears and wearing a grin like a wedge of Parmesan. Meanwhile more or less everyone else played to national stereotype. Dismal Gordon did his best to sound financially Churchillian, but succeeded only in seeming dead, while little Sarkozy jumped up and down saying 'non' in the hope that people would mistake him for de Gaulle.

The only one I liked was the frumpish Angela Merkel, who didn't seem to like anything. And who could blame her? The whole shebang begged for scoffery. As an economic summit it was risible. As anthropology it was fascinating. But essentially it was showbiz.

Here was the orgiastic red carpet of the Oscars, the intense analysis of frocks, the fawning interviews, the rifle fire of camera flashes and the fat fake smiles. Except, that is, in the back row of the group photograph where ignored South Americans muttered like banditos about the attention being paid to that bloated has-been called Europe.

The biggest of the big-wigs got to toddle along to Buck Pal to be blessed by the United Kingdom's highest priestess of juju, she of the violet frock and strangled vowels, and then everybody sat down to a banquet at Downing Street featuring a flock of dead Welsh lambs, cooked by Darling O'Camera himself, Jamie Bloody Oliver.

In other words, the whole thing was televisual. Its purpose was to bolster status and to wow the proles, to daunt by flaunting. And also to suggest that those in charge knew what they were doing and that what they were doing was to ensure that the rich bits of the globe stayed rich.

Most startling of all was Michelle Obama. She swept along to a girls' school in Islington chosen for its profusion of brown and black faces. There she expressed sentiments that would have seemed vapid and idealistic coming from the mouth of Miss World 1956. And how did the girlies respond to the carefully weighed sentiments of an unelected international stateswoman? They squealed. They gave her the same hormonal squeal that greeted the Beatles in the sixties, David Cassidy in the seventies, Madonna in the eighties and that then burst into tears over Princess Di. What we were witnessing was the next step in the canonisation of Sainte Michelle de Politico-Showbiz.

Another familiar ritual was played out on the streets. Every constable for miles around had his leave cancelled and was issued with body armour and a big stick. Then he went out to meet nice girls with quarter-baked notions of world peace, and a bunch of self-styled anarchists in anoraks. The anarchists expressed a desire to smash the system and to lynch a banker or two, though I doubt that any of them paid enough attention in Scouts to tie a serviceable noose.

They biffed bricks and hit a few windows but they missed the one fat and luscious irony, which was that the bankers they hated had got a sight closer to smashing the system than they had ever managed and all without taking their ties off. Rather than stringing them up they should have been toasting them.

Unless of course they were just testosterone-driven adolescent apes pretending to espouse a political cause for the sake of a nice bit of destruction. Which would make them into actors as well.

Tape ends

As soon as I read about the secret recordings of National Party MPs I knew immediately what had happened. My branch office in Washington had been burgled.

You may recall that some while ago my boffins perfected a tiny voice-activated transmitting microphone. I then employed pygmies with blowpipes to fire these mics at VIPs in the manner of vets tranquillising hippos. The results were sensational. I published off-the-record conversations featuring world leaders like David Beckham and Paris Hilton, and showbiz personalities like Tony Blair. I confidently expected many years of such scoops. But it's all over now, and it's Bill Gates' fault.

Having retired from Microsoft, Bill's not got much to do these days apart from wandering round Africa swatting tsetse flies. So he's taken to ringing me up. A few months back he called to congratulate me on single-handedly driving Mrs Snake-in-the-Cess-Pit Clinton out of the race for the White House. Bill then casually suggested that I ought to open a columnar office in Washington. And if by any chance I was interested, he knew of an office block going cheap. It belonged to, and was even named after, his brother Walter.

Well, I'm as much of a sucker for flattery as the next man. Moreover, the taped conversations that were pouring in from my transmitters all over the globe had just about swamped head office, aka my kitchen. Only the day before I had accidentally binned a priceless tape of Osama bin Laden ordering a burger in the Karachi branch of McDonald's. So I said yes.

Bill was delighted, of course. He himself undertook to set up a complex system of electronics that would reroute all the transmissions from my secret microphones and store them on cassette in Walter's office block. The system worked a treat. But I had forgotten, or perhaps, in my vanity, wilfully overlooked, the nature of Washington. It is a city without scruples. It is packed to the gunwales with thieves, scoundrels, ne'er-do-wells, loblollies and other elected officials. Within a month the National tapes emerged and I knew that I'd been burgled.

I flew straight over. A window had been jemmied, and the place ransacked. Every drawer lolled open like a dog's tongue. As I trudged from room to room my jandals scrunched on cassettes that the thieves had dropped as they fled. I took one as a souvenir, sold the office for half what I'd paid for it thanks to the sub-prime crisis — when sorrows come they come not single spies but in battalions — and flew home with the tape in my pocket and my heart in my boots.

I played the tape this morning. I don't think it's of any interest, but I have decided to publish it here as a reminder of the vanity of ambition.

It recorded a conversation between a man and a woman. They addressed each other as George and Condy.

Condy: Repeat after me, George, nu-cle-ar.

George: Nucular.

Condy: Oh come on, George, we've been working on this one for eight years now. NucLEar. It derives from the word nucleus.

George: Derives, Condy? Like derives a car?

Condy: Oh, forget it. What was it you wanted to see me about?

George: Just wanted to know what you thought of my speech in Thailand dissing the Chinks over human rights.

Condy: It's pronounced Tie-land, George.

George: Well, I'll be jiggered. But I saw some lovely thighs there, like the ones I patted on that beach volleyballer the other day. Gee, Laura was sore. But anyway, waddya think of my speech?

Condy: You mean apart from it being hypocritical?

George: Yeah, apart from that.

Condy: And apart from it being simplistic?

George: Yeah, apart from that.

Condy: And apart from it being a feeble attempt to sound like Kennedy in Berlin or even that old fraud Reagan?

George: Yeah, apart from that.

Condy: And apart from the plain bad manners of delivering such a speech before flying in to Beijing to watch the Olympics?

George: Gee, did you see them fireworks, Condy? Weren't they sumpin else?

Condy: And apart from its ignorance of 3000 years of Chinese civilisation?

George: That's enough 'apart froms', Condy. And tell me, if you're going to be snide, who was that dude I saw you with the other day? Short guy, double-breasted suit and a grin like a lighthouse. From Stralia or somewhere.

Condy: New Zealand, George. Complete lightweight, as it happens. But don't worry about him. He's last week's news, George, a bit like you. The world moves on, thank God.

George: Nuclear. I got it.

Condy: Too late, George, too bloody late.

A suitable note, I think, with which to end the last transcript that I shall ever publish from what I will always now think of as the Walter Gates tapes.

Lessons of the land

You've won and I've lost. I've started gardening. For real. So bravo. But please don't crow. Accept your victory with the good grace that the Australian cricket team, indeed any Australian sports team, indeed pretty well any sports team anywhere these days, doesn't.

(Am I alone in loathing the celebrations of a goal or a try or a wicket: the hooting and whooping and kissing and hugging, right in the face of the defeated? Perhaps I am. But watch footage of any cricket test before about 1975. When a wicket falls, there may be some shaking of hands. But then the players sit down and rest. They know they're just adults playing a game.)

So enjoy your victory, by all means, but don't rush round to your gardening neighbour waving this page in their face, screaming, 'Yoicks and caramba, we've won, the bugger has caved in' and offering a high five and a French kiss.

But you weren't going to, I know, because you gardeners have got things in perspective. Or rather, we gardeners have.

Why have I succumbed? Perhaps it was the gradual eroding effect of writing for this publication. Or else the depressing state of my garden. It was a ruin, a mess, a tumble of twitch and dankness with an understratum of dog bones. But mainly I blame Helen. Helen, the Trojan woman. She came to my house bearing gifts.

It wasn't my birthday or Christmas or Mother's Day or any of the other fake festivals promulgated by American corporations to give us yet one more excuse to seek unclutchable happiness through spending. It was just a Tuesday. And Helen turned up for no reason with a box. In the box a courgette seedling, a capsicum seedling, a tomato seedling, a cucumber seedling and a rose. A Margaret Merril. 'For your garden,' she said.

'But,' I said, and then I stopped. 'Thank you,' I said, keeping one hand firmly planted over the mouth of my curmudgeonliness. 'Thank you. You are kind.' And she was.

When Helen had gone, I went out and stood amid my twitch and dog bones and I thought, 'OK, all right, I'll try. It may be nice.' I fetched my grubber and spade and I went at it and got blisters but uncovered a formerly raised bed. The soil was like talcum powder so I drove to the garden centre and bought a bootload of organic rot in thumpingly inorganic plastic bags and lugged them home and up the steps.

When I regained the use of my spine, I kept going and uncovered more beds, what I think is an iris and a rockery. I started planting and I learned a lot of things quickly. And here, for your instruction, after six weeks of gardening, are those things.

That tomato seedlings die more or less immediately.

That capsicum seedlings and cucumber seedlings take longer.

That courgette seedlings don't die but neither do they grow.

That there is a direct correlation between the price of a

plant from the garden centre and the desire of a dog to bury a bone under it.

That there is an identical correlation between the efforts of a goat to pass through a fence and the cost of the plants on the other side.

That there were several weak spots in my fence.

That any planted seed germinates slower than any unplanted seed.

That the bright, descriptive tags on plants from the garden centre bear the same relation to the plants they describe as holiday brochures do to holidays.

That if the plants they describe were as durable as the tags, garden centres would go out of business.

That establishing a vegetable garden costs more than buying a greengrocer's.

That the best way to bring rain tomorrow is to water the garden today.

That the only way to discover where the previous occupant of this house laid an intricate system of irrigation is to put a spade through it.

That fennel is devil's spawn.

That the roots of fennel stretch to the centre of the earth.

That the roots of agapanthus make fennel roots seem puny.

That weeds can shoulder aside paving slabs.

That garden centre plants can shoulder aside nothing. A twig will buckle them.

That weeds can be distinguished from garden centre plants by use of a hoe. Wield the hoe in the standard manner for five minutes. The weeds are the plants still standing.

That jandals and a garden fork make a poor combination.

That the main purpose of doing work in the garden is to give a guided tour of it to visitors.

That visitor numbers dwindle rapidly.

And that the Margaret Merril is a thing of beauty and a joy for ever. And I want people to come round and admire it *now*.

Here's Y

This is spooky. I'm going to describe someone you know.

Uncommitted. Moving from job to job like a bee moving from flower to flower, taking whatever they can then buzzing on. Suspicious of all authority. Uninterested in politics. At ease with technology. Dismissive of people who aren't. Eager to travel. Seeing no point in a mortgage. Preferring to rent. Rootless and roofless.

Uncanny, isn't it? The description fits someone you know to that strangely flexible letter, a T. And that someone is young, aren't they, between the ages of 17 and 27. How do I do it?

Easy. I got it off someone else. He was a futurologist demographer or some such and he was addressing a conference. Inevitably he used PowerPoint. PowerPoint works on me like lunchtime Scotch, except that before sending me to sleep it doesn't make me jolly and garrulous, but I stayed awake long enough to work out what this man was doing. He was striking a sombre note to a middle-aged audience. He was putting up them that vertically invasive force, the wind.

His listeners were of the age that attends conferences, people with mortgages and pension plans, people who are not going to change jobs again, people with regulation haircuts and children and the dread that comes with middle age as they peep over the brow of the hill and see the north face of time descending into the inky valley of Was That It? The futurologist demographer was of a similar age but he was keen to demonstrate that he had stayed in touch with the zeitgeist. He knew and understood and even sometimes spoke to today's young. He would anatomise them for us. He called them Generation Y.

Or rather Generation Why. Why, ask the young, have you old people got old? Why have you turned crustier than a baguette? Why did you get into a rut and why have you stayed in it like agoraphobic moles? Why don't you buzz like bees across the flower meadow of the world? Why don't you let the winds of freedom blow through the hair you've no longer got? Why can't you work your BlackBerry?

The audience stirred uncomfortably. They did not want to be told that the young were restless, that the young were different, that the young were questioning things. They felt in their hearts the whispers of dread, like the rustling of brown paper in a breeze. Everything was threatened. The old certainties were dead. The futurologist looked pleased. It's sweet to be a prophet, sweeter still to preach doom.

But before we fret about Generation Y, let's consider the audience. They ranged in age from perhaps 30 to 70, and those aged 30 were dressed very similarly to those aged 70. Who were those 30-year-olds? They were Generation X.

Remember Generation X, whose pampered upbringing precluded their ever doing a decent day's work and whose indifference to everything would bring down the west? What were they doing at a conference? What indeed were they doing dressed at 11 in the morning? They should

61

have been lounging in bed waiting for breakfast to be served by their shuffling parents, who had devoted their lives to the cosseted cuckoos that they couldn't get out of the nest.

Yes, you might say, but there are always exceptions. Even the feckless Generation X would contain the odd kid who went right, who buckled down to reality, who was willing to work. Then let us consider the 50-year-olds at the conference, of whom I was one. Alphabetically I suppose we are Generation W. We were 20 in the seventies. We had hair we had to part in order to see the drugs we were buying. Our flared trousers could house families. We tuned in and dropped out and the old despaired of us. I remember a pub called The Bull where the gin ran as deep as the conservatism. Friends and I went there one night to laugh at the retired colonels in cravats. The landlord wore a regimental blazer. As we came through the door like inverted mops in cheesecloth shirts he emerged from behind his bar holding one hand aloft like a traffic policeman. 'Out!' he bellowed. 'Out!' We were bad and we were banned. For offending all the principles that he and the gin-soaked clientele had fought for. The colonels cheered as we withdrew.

And before us came Generation V, the 70-year-olds at the conference, the one-time teddy boys and mods and rockers and Elvis fans and do I need to go on? The young must question. It would be sad if they didn't. Generation Y is no different. And it is as sure as PowerPoint is soporific that they too will become middle-aged.

Up Lab Coat Ave

Hear that whirring? It's the noise of medical science backpedalling. Again.

Medical science is a good thing. It beavers away tirelessly in Lab Coat Avenue performing indignities on rats and thereby discovering all manner of stuff to sweeten my life. After a couple of thousand years and several billion rats its discoveries range from the simple aspirin to that most blessed of substances, Canesten cream. Thirty-five years ago, Canesten cured me of a dose of ringworm that threatened all adult pleasures. I remain grateful.

By comparison, theology, over the course of the same 2000 years, has managed to come up with the thumbscrew and 'Amazing Grace'. In other words, while theology has done its best to keep us mired in the swamp of superstitious suffering, medical science has done everything it can to haul us out. So thank you, medical science.

But medical science is far from infallible, and there remains one banana skin on which it comes a cropper as unfailingly as the Pope comes a cropper on condoms. That banana skin, that stumbling block, is the human diet.

The problem is that the human organism is neither consistent nor predictable. Inanimate substances are both. Add heat to magnesium, for example, and you will always get a laboratory full of excited schoolboys. Add heat to schoolboys, however, and who knows what will happen.

And on the matter of diet, the denizens of Lab Coat Avenue simply have no idea how it works. For evidence take the placebo effect. We ingest something that shouldn't affect us and it affects us.

The active ingredient seems to be belief. If you believe that something will do you good, it does you good. Presumably the mind deceives the body. But the mind is part of the body. So does the mind somehow deceive itself? I don't know, and neither, obviously, does medical science.

Just about the only dogmatic statement you can make about diet is that you can't make any dogmatic statement about it. If someone with terminal cancer believes a pork sausage will cure them, there's a chance that it may.

And yet, in defiance of all this, Lab Coat Avenue insists on making dogmatic pronouncements about diet. It bellows these pronouncements from the roof of the lab. And then, a decade later, it retracts them rather more quietly.

Think back 10 years to that benighted period when the myth of deep vein thrombosis was terrorising air travellers. At the time, what was dietary enemy number one, the newly discovered Lord High Executioner? You could be tested for it in little stalls set up in shopping malls. Remember now? That's right, cholesterol. Cholesterol killed. It clogged the arteries and slit the thin-spun life. Eat eggs and die soon. Eat butter and die now.

Last night in the pub I heard about a man who liked eggs. Aged 50 or so, he suffered a minor heart attack. The doctor, in accordance with the diktats of Lab Coat Ave, put him on a low cholesterol diet. He was allowed one egg a week. The man trusted his doc and stuck miserably to his egg limit. He died.

Now, it is possible that his weekly egg killed him. But it is every bit as possible that the dearth of eggs killed him. The body is a creature of habit and this man was accustomed to eating eggs by the clutch. But the most probable truth is that the diet made no difference at all to his health. For from the moment the world learned that cholesterol was the ultimate enemy, medical science has been retracting that assertion bit by bit.

First came the division into good cholesterol and bad cholesterol. We were supposed to distinguish between saturated fats and non-saturated fats and poly-unsaturated fats and trans-gender fats and I don't know and don't care what else.

Then came the anomalies. Some people, it seemed, lived off bleached broccoli wrapped in raw cabbage and yet had cholesterol levels that soared like Concorde at take-off. Whereas others lived off chocolate, cream, eggs and chocolate cream eggs and yet had arteries like well-reamed rifles.

Then finally, just this week, the lab coats fessed up. Eggs are just dandy, they said. Go ahead, they said, eat as many as you like. And also, by the way, and sorry for misleading you, there is no establishable correlation between cholesterol in the diet and cholesterol clogging the arteries. None. None whatsoever. Zero. Zilch.

Furthermore, there is evidence that having high blood cholesterol may be a good thing. Cholesterol, like smoking, may ward off dementia.

The sum total of this is that it doesn't much matter what

we eat. We are omnivores. If we eat too much we get fat. If we eat nothing we die, though it takes a while. In between those two extremes pretty well anything goes. The vital thing is not to worry about it. Worry kills. Cholesterol doesn't.

Encouraging and true

The political significance of the following story may not be immediately apparent.

The woman, a friend of mine, sank onto the sofa with the involuntary sigh that denotes the end of the day. All her duties were done. Ahead of her lay only the slow dwindle towards bed. Every evening is like a little death.

She flicked through some television channels, found nothing but scabrous trash, reached for a novel on the coffee table, then froze. For she had discovered that she was not alone. On the cushion next to her, and apparently snoozing, sat a substantial spider.

I have known people who at this point would flee the house, leap into a car, roar down the drive with their eyes on the rear-view mirror in case the beast was following, pull up at the real estate agency and put the house on the market. One such person I knew went on to become an All Black. But this woman is not such a person.

Nevertheless, like most of us, she did not feel entirely at ease sharing her furniture with a chunky spider. I cling to a theory that we dislike spiders because the arch of their legs reminds us of the McDonald's logo. The theory is nonsense but I enjoy the clinging.

(I learned recently, by the bye, that Mr Warren Buffett, the American who became a billionaire not by doing anything new or clever or beautiful, but simply by buying shares and not selling them — and who is often referred to as the Sage of Omaha, sagacity these days being measured in dollars — subsists on a diet of hamburgers, fries and cherry-flavoured Coke. Such food is America's third greatest contribution to the infantilisation of the west. (The first and second place-getters, respectively, are Hollywood and grievance litigation.) Nevertheless, the point needs to be made that despite his lifelong consumption of baby food, Sage Buffett has reached the age of approximately 200 years. His longevity confirms, yet again, that lifespan is by and large a lottery, that the human gut is stout and adaptable, and that the nutritional faddists and five-plus-a-day bullies are as wrong as New Zealand First.)

I don't know whether Mr Buffett has a kind heart, but the woman on the sofa has. And she is especially sympathetic to animals. Had she been born in India she would have become a Jainist. Jainists are so eager to preserve the life of even the meanest creature that they sweep the path ahead of them with a brush of soft twigs.

Anyway, Ms Kindheart went to the kitchen to fetch a jar. As she returned to the sofa, she worried briefly that when she tried to capture the spider it might spit venom into her eyes, blind her, send her reeling across the room and blundering into furniture until she fell, whereupon it would saunter over at its leisure and feast on her flesh, sucking the fluids out until . . . but it didn't. Indeed it tumbled into the jar with only a little urging from a rolled magazine. She screwed down the lid, then fetched a drill from the garage to make air holes. She is, I repeat, Ms Kindheart.

While the spider examined its puzzling transparent cage she examined the spider. In the region where a tail would be it sported a prominent blob of white. White-tailed spiders are Australian and poisonous — a pair of adjectives that are not of necessity synonyms.

When her husband returned late from work he found the jar on the bench with a Post-it note saying 'White-tailed spider?' He went to bed. He knows his wife well.

Over breakfast the next morning she raised the subject of the spider. Her husband suggested that they kill it. His wife, who is almost as realistic as she is kind-hearted, eventually agreed. But there remained the decision on how to do the deed. Husband favoured stamping on it. His wife did not. She said to leave it with her.

That evening, when the husband fetched a bottle of unoaked chardonnay from the fridge, he was surprised to find it alongside the jar with the spider in it. Over dinner, and with studied casualness, he brought the subject up once more.

'Ah yes,' she said, 'I meant to tell you. I did some research, you see. The kindest way to kill insects is to freeze them.'

The husband made to speak but paused first to spear a forkful of steak. It was a trick that marriage had taught him. He chewed. Then, 'But it won't freeze in the fridge.'

'I know,' said his wife, 'but I thought that freezing would come as less of a shock if I chilled it first.' So saying, she stood and opened the freezer door and popped the spider in to die.

And the political significance? Well, in sharp distinction to the recent election campaign the story is both encouraging and true.

How I did good

I didn't expect a Nobel Prize but it would have been nice to be thanked. I had, after all, done the world some service. For with a series of columns published in this very paper I explained to the great American public that Hillary Clinton was a snake in the grass and persuaded them not to let her stash her tangerine trouser suits in the White House wardrobe, or her silver-haired, silver-tongued smarm of a hubby. It would have been nice to be thanked.

To my surprise, however, and despite the letters of gratitude that didn't come pouring into my letter box, I found that I enjoyed the sensation of doing good. And while the feeling lasted, while I was still oozing benevolence like a wounded Pope, I resolved to keep going. I would sort out more of the world's problems.

I began my mission at the bar. 'Come on,' I said, to the usual band of topers and wastrels, 'out with it. What's driving you to drink? What's troubling you?'

They mumbled into their tumblers.

'The drinks are on me,' I said. 'All I ask in return is the reason for your distress. Hand over your grief to Uncle Joe. Didn't I single-handedly keep Ms Snake in the Grass from the White House?'

They couldn't deny it.

'So come on then,' I said, 'tell me what's wrong with the world.'

Then out it came, a torrent of distress, pouring from the larynxes of Mr and Mrs Ordinary Sot. I listened, I nodded and I took notes.

'The world is dirty, dirty,' said one from deep in his gin. 'And it's all our fault. We've soiled our own nest, ruined a place that was once green and pleasant.'

'And now the planet is heating up,' said another. 'Unstoppably. Our children are going to fry, fry, do you hear me?'

'I hear you,' I said.

'And what children!' wailed a raddled madam. 'Just look at them. They've got so fat. Every class used to have its fat child, but now there are thousands of them, thousands of lurching lardy wobbleguts. Kids have a duty to be sleek and beautiful. There's time enough to be fat later in life,' and here she peeped ruefully down at what looked like a stack of motorbike tyres crammed into her Merino top, 'but in youth, oh, even I was graceful and slender, an emblem of the beauty that is inherent in our species. What's gone wrong?'

Before I could sympathise, a bearded man spoke. 'The ladies and gentlemen too much alone,' he said, quoting the poet Auden with impressive accuracy considering the Pernods he had lowered at my expense. 'Where once was connection, now there is isolation. No one knows his neighbours. The simple pleasures of human relations have been replaced by internet porn. There will always be misery, but once there was consolation in community. We were all in this together. Now we are all in this alone.'

'Shopping,' screamed a hitherto silent woman. 'Shopping. Behold the malls. Great consumptive cathedrals set in acres of car park, to which the millions throng every weekend. They are trying to buy joy. But they find that joy is like an eel. They flash the credit card and think they've got joy by the gills, but then it wriggles and is gone.'

'Enough,' I said, 'you have spoken and I have heard.'

Paying the bill with a magisterial swipe of the EFTPOS, I left the soaks to soak further. Burdened with the weight of their grief, I went home to think. Within minutes thought had become action. I registered on line as a futures trader. And I bought oil. Sweet Brent crude, Taranaki Heavy, Alberta Tar Sands derivatives, I bought the lot. I drove them up. Others followed my lead. Soon there was panic in the exchanges. At 140 smackers a barrel, I cashed in and quietly left the market, trillions of dollars richer, but knowing I had done a very good thing.

For with the price of petrol doubling the bulbous children will now have to walk to school or P lab, and the streets will grow slippery with the fat they shed. Meanwhile the traffic on those streets will dwindle to a trickle of public transport. Forsaking their beloved cars, which consume a third of the world's fuel, people will use their local shops where they will meet their neighbours and discover that they can be friends. The giant suburban malls will crumble to dust. Trees will sprout in the car parks. And as the exhaust fumes cease, the skies will brighten. The planet will begin to lick itself clean like a cat and temperatures will stabilise. And all manner of things shall be well.

It is a fine thing that I did. I'm looking forward to being thanked.

Showdown mit Gott

Islam met Christianity last week. The showdown took place on a football pitch in Berlin. The referee was a rabbi. Two younger Jews ran the touchline. Among the spectators was the Prince of Wales. The football match was the idea of the Reverend Christopher Jage-Bowler, 47, a former champagne salesman for Moët & Chandon. I am not making any of this up. In this wonderful world of ours, I never have to.

The match attracted a lot of advance media attention but little regard was paid to the football itself. So I shall now start making it up.

'All that hype about a rerun of the Crusades is in pretty poor taste,' said the Christians' manager, Archbishop Beard, before the game. 'We've tried not to allow it to get to us. And all credit to the boys, they realise this is only a friendly. Both teams are guaranteed a place in the first division of the world cup in perpetuity, so there's really nothing to play for. The days of grudges and ancient inter-tribal feuds being played out on the sports pitches of the world are long gone. The hatchet has been well and truly buried by universal prosperity and mutual respect.'

'Hear hear,' said Ayatollah Biggabeard, 'any thought of the time when European armies descended on our ancestral homelands under the banner of a religion of peace to plunder and slaughter and to cause the blood to run like a river through the streets of Tyre and Acre, could not be further from our minds. We are just looking forward to a good clean game, insh'allah, may his name be a blessing.' And the two managers shook hands cordially and hugged, then missed the first few minutes of the game while they disentangled their beards.

Kicking off into an apathetic wind, the Christians strove to keep the ball in midfield, but were hampered by schisms. Hours of ecumenical training did not seem to pay off as the Copts passed the ball among themselves in an old-fashioned manner and kept possession away from any team-mates domiciled west of Constantinople. The Vatican Pope, one of the few Christians bent on attack, and running with an energy that belied his veteran status, kept calling for the ball on the right, but the Copts failed to recognise him.

The situation was mirrored for the Islamists where their explosive far-left winger was largely ignored by a packed if passive midfield. A small but vocal minority on the terraces were heard to chant 'Give it to Laden', but they were drowned out by the mainstream.

As a contest the match threatened to subside into a genteel kickabout with neither side wishing to threaten the other's goal. Until, that is, the Christian winger, a Texan Baptist who'd been insistently bellowing for the ball, made a raid infield. With a cry of 'That's for 9/11' he lunged at an imam with his studs raised. As the imam writhed on the ground, Ref Rabbi reached into his pocket and withdrew a red card. Uproar.

'Who's kept Israel supplied with military hardware since 1948?' screamed the Texan, his features turning puce. 'Come on, Jewboy, answer me that. Without us the heathens would have tossed you out of the Middle East in minutes and spit-roasted your children.'

The referee hesitated. His red card wavered. Players gathered round the ref and jostling began.

The Christians' goalkeeper, meanwhile, a substantial Carmelite nun, had run upfield to tend to the stricken imam. As she knelt beside him and laid a hand on his wounded leg, a mullah, sprinting towards the Texan and the ref with the traditional Afghan enthusiasm for a stoush of any sort, tripped over her. He fell. She screamed. The Vatican Pope rushed to her side. The Texan hurled abuse. The Islamic left winger came dashing in from the touchline. A group of mountain-dwelling Pakistani spectators leapt the crash barriers and followed him. Before they could reach the Texan they were met by a tour party from South Carolina who were in the mood for a bit of biffo since having their inflammatory banners confiscated at the turnstiles. Fists flew. Around the fringes of the affray several Church of England vicars stood wringing their hands crying, 'Stop, please, stop. We're all friends here.'

'Oh no we're not, you lily-livered Limeys,' screamed a South Carolina pastor, swinging a huge and joyous haymaker that flattened an Iranian scholar, and laid out one of the vicars on the follow through.

At this point the entire crowd of approximately 3 billion surged onto the pitch, any thought of a football game was abandoned and the fight went on most happily for days.

'I think it would be fair to say,' said the Prince of Wales, who, when he eventually ascends the throne, wishes to be known as the defender of faiths, 'that the game was not a success. But I can't quite put my finger on why.'

75

The Beast

'Foxtrot Elim to Mission Control, are you reading me? Over.'

'Foxtrot Elim, this is Mission Control. Provide sitrep. Over.'

'All quiet. Access impeded by dense vegetation. Request permission to proceed. Over.'

'Proceed with caution, repeat caution. Intelligence suggests imminent hostile threat. Likely presence of one civilian. Probably intense emotional condition. Priority evacuation. Air back-up available. Do not, repeat not, engage enemy unless essential. Is that understood, Foxtrot Elim, repeat, is that . . .?'

Slowly, like a mushroom sprouting, a helmet rose above the swaying grass stems. The platoon commander whistled softly. Three other helmets rose, also like mushrooms sprouting, above the swaying grass stems. Three unshaven faces, grimly set, jaws tense, cheeks daubed with camouflage paint peered across the tops of the swaying grass stems towards the platoon commander. With a click like the flicking of fingers the platoon commander released the safety catch on his weapon. Above the rustle of swaying grass stems, three echoing clicks.

'Foxtrot Elim, Foxtrot Elim. Do not engage, repeat, do not engage.'

With a barely perceptible nod of his helmet, the

commander motioned his men forward. They crawled up the steep slope like lizards until they came in sight of a building and stopped. They lay still, very still.

Then on the breeze, faintly, from behind the house, 'Back, I tell you, back.' The voice was close to hysterical. With it came repeated thwacks and swipes, increasing in intensity, in ferocity, in tempo. 'No, get back, get back. I shall not cede.'

'Foxtrot Elim, Foxtrot Elim, are you reading me? Over.'

'Reading you loud and clear, Mission Control. We're going in. Over and out.'

The platoon commander stood. His men stood. Up the slope they ran, through the chest-high swaying grass stems. The cries of the desperate civilian grew more frantic, higher in pitch. 'No,' it screamed, 'no no no no.' The soldiers caught sight of him, encircled by vegetation that reared around and above him like a green hydra, a hydra that grew larger as they watched, that in seconds it seemed would engulf the man, his car, his house, his life. At the base of the great vegetable beast there sprouted truncheons of fibrous flesh, swelling like long green balloons, spiking the air, massive, obscene, predominant. The man was flailing, screaming, ululating. The platoon commander just had time to notice a dog cowering in the corner of the yard, too scared even to bark, then 'Charge,' he bellowed.

The commandos charged. Firing from the hip as they ran, they poured magazine after magazine into the heart of the swelling beast. Sap flew, pith spattered. The plant reared and writhed and in the kinaesthetic confusion of battle seemed to roar like a bull. And as it roared it extruded ever more truncheons, all of them swelling unstoppably. The platoon commander burst through the outer vegetation, seized the civilian, flung him over his shoulder and tried to withdraw. But a vast and crinkled leaf, bristling like a leg shaved three days ago, rasped at his face, his torso. Bullets from the covering commandos shredded the leaf at the very moment it threatened to rip the machine gun from the commander's grasp. The commander burst free and took shelter behind the house.

He laid the civilian down beside the council wheelie bin marked 'Green Waste'. He slapped the man's cheeks. No response. The dog sidled over, its tail whipped between its legs like an inverted question mark, and licked the man's face. His eyes opened.

'No no no no,' he jabbered, swinging his arms about him as if besieged by flies, 'back back.' The dog recoiled.

'It's all right,' said the platoon commander roughly, shaking the man by the shoulders. 'We're here. You're safe. It's OK. We'll kill it.'

'One,' stammered the man, 'I just got one, I thought one would be OK. Holy Mary Mother of God, bless us now and in the time of . . .' and his words subsided into incoherence.

'Foxtrot Elim, Foxtrot Elim, this is Mission Control. Am sending in air support.'

'Take cover,' yelled the platoon commander.

A squadron of fighter jets ramped over the horizon. Three commandos flung themselves down beside their commander, the jabbering civilian and the terrified dog. All covered their heads with their hands, apart from the dog, who used his paws.

On the instant all was smoke and noise and chaos. The

aircraft swooped and turned and swooped again. The men did not know how long they lay there. When the planes had gone and the smoke cleared, they rose tentatively to survey a new and utterly different world.

'Foxtrot Elim, Foxtrot Elim.'

'This is Foxtrot Elim. Mission accomplished. Enemy destroyed. Over.'

And as the civilian sat with his arm around his dog, his eyes so widely open they spoke of long counselling sessions to come, the soldiers set about cramming into the wheelie bin the tattered remains of a single zucchini plant.

On the buses

It was horrible and it was on a bus. I wasn't. I was following the bus in my car, which is as close as I like to get to public transport. Buses are ghastly. You only have to look at the sallow people on board to realise that they are passing germs around like a plate of pikelets.

When I was young, poor and careless, I caught buses without a second thought. But back then everyone knew the name of every germ going and had built up immunity to them like the walls round Carcassonne. Measles? Had it. Mumps? Had it. Erectile dysfunction? Don't talk dirty.

But now, ha. Every day brings a new germy threat that can waltz unchallenged past the immunity guards and set up shop in the city of the human heart and start cultivating lumps or dissolving one's intestines. I know so because I read the *Sunday Star-Times*. And on wintry afternoons you can see those germs breeding inside buses with such terrible fecundity that they mist up the windows.

As it happens, the horrible thing I saw on the bus wasn't a germ, and I'll get round to it in a minute, but first I want to mention a survey I read last week. Yes, I know, surveys are dismal things. They are fake news for newsless days. The results are acquired by asking the sort of people who respond to surveys what they think about some issue of national importance — the sex habits of game show hosts, say — collating what the respondents think, most of which is actually what they think they ought to think or want to be seen thinking, and then reporting the fatuous results back to them as if those results came straight from the printing press of the Almighty, piping hot and dripping truth. A recent survey, for example, and one that became an item on the evening news, revealed that the average Kiwi eats, drinks and sleeps a lot, and that these things make him happy. As revelations go, this is on a par with a survey I have conducted in the last five seconds, which has revealed that the average Kiwi is the proud owner of just under two legs.

But the survey I read last week was exquisite. I don't know who paid for it. You and I, probably, in the form of rates, but for once I don't mind. The survey asked the citizens of Christchurch what they thought of their public transport system and the citizens of Christchurch reported that they were very proud of it. They thought it was clean, reliable, constantly improving, safe, cheap and in all ways a credit to the city. But they didn't use it.

Of course they don't use it. A car beats the bus every time. A car is warm and private. It departs when you want it to, and it goes where you want it to. You can smoke in it, sing in it, fart in it. The bus just can't compete. Except, that is, as a medium for advertising. Buses are big and they're always on the move so they make splendid billboards. Which brings us, at last, to the horrible thing. It was an ad for TV3 News on the back of a bus.

It showed two men on a hill in what may have been Afghanistan. One of the men was a soldier. The other, who was holding a microphone, was that most puzzling of modern celebrities, a television newsreader. To illustrate how thoroughly he'd assimilated local culture, the newsreader was wearing a chequered cotton scarf. So far so horrible.

But it was the caption that made me shrivel. 'It's all about the story,' it said, at which point I had better pause while you dash to the bathroom with your hand over your mouth, lean into the basin and then clean yourself up.

All done? Good.

I have written about 'it's all about' before. 'At best,' I wrote, 'the phrase means "here's something I like". When used in a speech it operates like a premonitory cough, warning the audience of the approach of something platitudinous but clappable. "It's all about integrity." '

Now, one expects platitudinous tosh from politicians. They are in the business of arousing emotion and obscuring the truth. The news media, however, are in precisely the opposite business. Their job is to override emotion and to expose the truth. Their medium for doing so is language. So when, as here, you find a news organisation, which should be a champion of precise, incisive language, using the shoddy, colloquial meaninglessness of 'it's all about' simply in order to evoke a favourable emotional reaction and thereby garner more viewers, which will in turn enable it to charge more for the advertising it depends on, advertising that outdoes even the politicos in its desire to arouse emotion and obscure the truth, well, it's enough to make a bloke board a bus and take a good deep breath.

IYP to IYR

On New Year's Eve fireworks will erupt from the rich bits of the globe to light up whatever 2009 has in store for global capitalism. The party will be boisterous. But take a moment to kneel and put your ear to the ground. Behind the bangs and squeals, the kissings and the Auld Lang Synes, you may just catch the thud of falling fabric. That's the curtain coming down on the International Year of the Potato.

What a year it's been. The International Year of the Potato (IYP) germinated in March 2007 when the Food and Agriculture Organisation (FAO) of the United Nations (UN) in New York (NY) established an Informal International Steering Committee (IISC) and gave it a mission for 2008: to raise potato awareness (PA).

It is amazing what human beings can achieve with dedication, belief and an expense account. The official launch of the IYP took place in New York just seven months later. The guest list sparkled: lofty UN officials, the entire IISC (and partners), UN delegates from all over the world, and countless representatives of the global potato community, all of them bent on a binge. It is rumoured that the event was even attended by the Secretary General of the Committee Responsible for Acronym Proliferation (which is always referred to as the Committee Responsible for Acronym Proliferation).

But by far the most important guests were 300 lucky

83

schoolchildren from Washington DC. At first glance it seems odd that children were bussed in from Washington when there must have been plenty available in New York. But one should never doubt a steering committee. I am confident they'd done their research and found that the young of New York had a high Potato Awareness factor, whereas the young of Washington didn't.

The children's parents were not invited. From the outset the IYP was focused on the future, and though those parents may well have peeled, boiled, roasted, fried or mashed potatoes every day of their lives, they are too old to become properly potato aware.

It was a belter of a bash. The UN offices still buzz with stories of the hangovers acquired. And from then on the IYP sprouted everywhere. There were potato-themed art competitions, potato cooking competitions and a global potato photo competition. If you want to know who won, you can find out on the IYP's comprehensive official website www.potato2008.org. On that website you'll marvel at the IYP logo (several glowing potato-like blobs) and you'll learn pretty well all there is to learn about 'the honest potato', a phrase they use to distinguish it from less trustworthy tubers.

You will learn that the potato was first cultivated in the Andes some 8000 years ago, and that the tireless committee lugged their credit cards down to Peru many times over the course of the IYP to get right to the heart of Potato Awareness. There they discovered that farmers celebrate the coming potato crop by throwing coloured ribbons over their fields, and on the IYP website you can see a photo of a happy Andean woman doing exactly that. You can also watch a video that lays stress on the special relationship that has always existed between women and potatoes.

Right now the IYP is winding down with a month of celebrations in Rome, a city that has always underachieved in Potato Awareness because of its affection for pasta. So on 11 December more than 350 Roman schoolchildren took a guided tour of a Potato Exhibition in FAO's glass-domed atrium. They learned about the potato's history, its nutritional benefits and its social and cultural significance. I bet those bambini were the envy of their classmates.

On 12 December the IISC of the IYP gathered to review the year's achievements and three days after that they came together once more to celebrate the publication of *New light on a hidden treasure*, a 144-page illustrated book that is bound for the top of the bestseller charts. It records the achievements of the International Year of the Potato. The book is available in Arabic, Chinese, English, French, Russian and Spanish.

So much achieved in one short year. But in a couple of weeks it will all be over. A line will be drawn under the expense accounts, the IYP credit cards will be blocked, the steering committee will bid each other tearful farewells and then there will be an almighty scrummage as they battle with the website builders, the videographers and the translators to leap aboard the next gravy train departing from UN Central. It should have room for most of them: 2009 is officially the International Year of Reconciliation.

Which is good news for the world's poor. During 2009 they will learn to reconcile themselves to the fact that they ended the International Year of the Potato exactly as they began it, acutely aware that they had no potatoes to eat.

O Holy Co

'O Holistic Wellness Coach,' I said, 'may I ask you some questions?'

'Of course,' said the Holistic Wellness Coach in his deep Canadian voice. 'But let's drop the formality. Call me Holy Co, my friend. Now how can I help?'

'O Holy Co, for reasons that need not concern us, a Canadian friend has just sent me your book about how to achieve holistic wellness.'

'And how did you find it?'

'I just looked in the mail box,' I said. 'And because I have never read anything from the Mind, Body and Spirit section of a bookshop before, I fair sprinted to my study and opened your book with fingers a-tremble and became so engrossed that I ingested every word of the introduction before running to the bathroom.'

'My son,' purred Holy Co, 'you have started down the golden road to holistic health. Soon you will radiate wellness and when people ask you the secret you will recommend my book to them. You shall become well in mind, body and spirit. And I shall become rich. So how can I help?'

'Well, Holy Co, you say that certain "progressive health and lifestyle practices" such as veganism and "new definitions of personal spirituality through global integrative approaches to faith" were "greeted with derision" only a couple of decades ago.'

'Yes, sadly, they were.'

'And they still are, Holy Co. By me. I'm a greeter-with-derision. I'm so sorry. Is there any hope of my ever being well?'

'It won't be easy,' said Holy Co, and I could hear the sadness in his voice. 'You will have to go on a long journey.'

'I've already started, Holy Co,' I exclaimed. 'From your introduction I have learnt that the first step to holistic wellness "is to ensure our health of mind, as it is our mind that mediates our physical activity and helps to frame our spiritual life".'

'Very good.'

'Yes, but can you please clarify what you mean when you say that the mind mediates physical activity? Do you just mean that in order, say, to raise two fingers to a wellness coach, I first have to decide to do it? I know I'm slow, but I do like to get things straight so we both know what we're talking about.

'And while you're at it, can you please explain exactly how my mind "helps to frame" my spiritual life? I don't think I've got a spiritual life, framed or unframed, but I want one. And if the mind only helps in the framing process, what else is involved? What additional framer do I need in order to get my spiritual framing done?

'I desperately need to know because in the same paragraph you explain that the spiritual life "ultimately shapes the overall health of our entire being"?

'I'm impressed, of course, by the use of ultimately, overall and entire in the one clause, three absolute terms that underline the primacy of the spiritual life, but I still haven't got things quite clear. You see, if the mind, along with one or more other unspecified framing agencies, frames the spiritual life, how does the spiritual life then turn the tables and start shaping the health of our entire being, which, as you repeatedly stress, is an amalgam of mind, body and spirit?

'In other words, how does a thing that's been partially framed by a second thing then turn around and shape the health of the second thing, and of itself, and of a third thing which, as I'm sure I don't need to remind you, is mediated by the second thing? Do I make myself clear?'

'My poor benighted son.'

'Hold it one moment, Holy Co,' I said, 'I'm almost done. Then you can put everything straight in one go. Can you please explain how it is that I, who have the spiritual life of a plastic bag, and whose mind runs on a high octane fuel of rage and scorn at the scams that are practised on the gullible by the manipulative, all of which ought to mean, according to you, that I am sick as a dog, am practically always well? (And so is my dog.) For in 30 something years of a working life I have had only a dozen days off, two of which were for broken bones, three for tonsillitis, one for bee stings, and the rest were sickies thrown because reprobate mates turned up unexpectedly with a wish to go on a bender. And finally can you explain, if you are so concerned about my well-being, and if, as you insist, selfless generosity is essential to wellness of mind, body and spirit, why you don't sell your book to the unwell masses for exactly what it's worth, which is nothing?'

'Sorry,' said Holy Co. 'Got to get to the bank.'

Thanks, mole

Did you think there were no moles in New Zealand? Well, you were wrong. I've got a pet one and I love him. The mole is a fish of the earth. It rows through the soil hunting worms. Its whiskers can detect an idling earthworm at a distance of several metres, whereupon the mole burrows towards it, seizes it, wrestles it into submission, squeezes the soil from its gut and then stores it in an underground larder for later consumption, and all in the time it takes you or me to read a medium-length novel. It's a fine life.

My mole, however, is neither subterranean nor vermivorous. He's only metaphorically a mole. He's a Wellington bureaucrat who from time to time sends me stuff written by other Wellington bureaucrats. Recently he sent me the following press release. He insists he did not make it up.

'With Daylight Saving having come to an end, the Department of Labour is reminding people to look out for workers working in dim evening light, as this will now be more likely with increasing hours of darkness, as we move into winter . . .

'We should be on the lookout for a number of workers, ranging from children delivering junk mail, newspaper deliverers, couriers, and road workers and — of course — those who are working within their normal workplaces in diminished light conditions.

'People need to remember that as well as places such as

loading zones, warehouses, car parks and marshalling areas where light may be reduced, roads and footpaths are often workplaces too. We need to consider the needs of those who work there and take care not to put them in danger. If we collectively increase our awareness, that will prevent accidents, injuries and even deaths.'

Well now, what did you make of that? Exactly. Me too. I want a job writing this sort of thing.

For at 52 years old I'm through with selfishness. I itch to give something back, to do a little good. And what greater good could I do than to raise awareness of danger?

My problem is how to get the job. If I knew the author's name, I could, I suppose, seize him, wrestle him into submission, squeeze the soil from his gut, steal his clothes, stroll into his office, say good morning to his secretary and call for tea and biscuits while I go about my danger-awareness-raising mission. But I don't know his name, so I have decided to apply directly to his employers. And in order to convince them of my fitness for the job I have spent the day knocking up some press releases.

'The arrival in this country of a container vessel loaded with discounted Ecuadorian bananas has caused the Department of Labour to issue a yellow alert.

'Director of Safety, Joe Bennett, says that the influx of cheap fruit raises the spectre of a potential banana skin disposal problem situation.

'The slipperiness of discarded banana skins is well attested,' says Mr Bennett, 'and some sectors of society are especially vulnerable. Vigilance is urged on all workers whose employment is likely to bring them into contact with the elderly or with circus clowns. In particular all rest homes catering specifically to elderly circus clowns will be issued with a supply of emergency banana skin disposal bags.'

See? Not just a vague warning to raise awareness, but practical steps to avert the danger.

Or how about this one?

'Statistics from ACC have revealed a startling increase in pyjama-related injuries. Over the last year the number of men who have inserted both legs into the same leg of their pyjamas and then fallen over has skyrocketed by 100 per cent. Approximately half of the victims were hospitalised. The other one recuperated at home.

'Department of Labour Supreme Director General of Safety Awareness (staff 213 and growing), Joe Bennett, says it would be irresponsible to ignore this epidemic. Planning is already in an advanced stage for a pyjama awareness road show to tour the nation's secondary schools. Meanwhile as a matter of urgency a bill has been introduced to raise the minimum age of pyjama purchase and to require retailers to attach a prominent warning notice to all pyjamas.'

Or, and this is surely the clincher: 'Attention is drawn to the danger of safety warning fatigue,' announces Global Safety Director of the UN, His Excellency Sir Joseph Bennett, from his throne in New York. 'The proliferation of safety warnings throughout the western world has led to diminishing returns and in some cases even active hostility. In consequence His Excellency has had no choice but to authorise the mobilisation of a nuclear-armed multinational peacekeeping force, and grant them emergency powers to seize, squeeze and destroy anyone not complying with safety directives issued from this office. The only way to escape is to live underground and eat worms.'

Playing nice

Rafa versus Roger. It should have been no contest. The name Rafa sparkles. It suggests raffish, and you have to like raffish. There's also an echo of Raffles, the stylish crook. Whereas Roger, with that pudding of an O at its heart, is a name like suet, plain and heavy. I can think of no one exciting called Roger, though the name has become a synonym for bonk.

I watch tennis about as often as I shoot dogs, but I have just watched the last set of the Wimbledon men's final and it held me like a vice.

It held the crowd too. After almost five hours of tennis the crowd was still in thrall, chanting between points, gasping during them. It was a primal contest and we all love a primal contest. We identify with one or the other man, see him as representative of qualities we like, and urge him to conquer the qualities we don't like. It's us against them, tribe against tribe, an election with balls. It doesn't matter but it seems to matter. It's serious play. Serious play is unserious war.

The contrast between these men was exquisite, almost epochal. Roger Federer chose to be Edwardian. He arrived on court in flannel trousers and a cream cardigan. It was pure 1911.

When he stripped off the flannels and cardy, he became pure convention. Here was the plain white polo shirt, the top button undone but the middle one done. His shorts stopped at the currently correct distance above the knee. His clothes just said 'tennis player' then they shut up and let Roger get on with being one.

Rafa Nadal was today and himself. His clothes insisted on difference. His shorts were long, stretching to the knee, suggestive of beaches. His shirt was a muscle-T, the sleeves aborted to reveal arms. And what arms. His humped brown biceps seem to have independent life. And he loved them. Between games, and even between points, he towelled them adoringly. He had the vanity of a young man who is surprised and delighted by what puberty has made of him.

There is something simian about Rafa, something anthropoidal. He has an eyebrow ridge like those mock-ups of cavemen in museum dioramas. And he grunted on court. His every service, every top-spun pass, every thunderous drive, came with an involuntary ugh of exertion. And before he served, his right hand snuck behind him and twitched the cloth from between his buttocks, a private furtive act for most of us, but for him just unselfconscious male physicality.

Opposite him stood the urbane Roger, who would no more twitch his shorts from his bum cleft than he would stab his grandmother. Roger is contained. He may want to weep but he does not weep. He may want to scream but he does not scream. Screaming and weeping are unseemly, indecent. For we are adults, aren't we, and we just don't, do we?

But you could see in his shots the ferocity of his endeavour. He drove his forehand into the far corner like the thrust of a sword, a thin fast murderous sword, a blade. And as he drove it home he skipped, both feet off the ground, his body unfurling like a cracked whip. His emotion was channelled into the discipline of technique. It found no other outlet. If he missed an easy shot he would just raise an eyebrow in self-disgust, briefly. If he won a big point he just clenched his fingers close to his heart, briefly.

But not Rafa. Rafa would shout and uppercut the air, once, twice, three times, with that young man's fist and those piston biceps. He held nothing back. He gave.

Restraint versus disinhibition. A turning inward against a bellowing outward. Cultured against primitive. Adult against adolescent. For Roger had won the last five championships, but now a new young lion was roaring on his patch. Would the old order change? Would the alpha male be driven from the pride? Who would get mating rights?

The camera swung often to Roger's girlfriend, or perhaps wife. She was not the blonde dolly that so often latches on to sporting stars, but a more womanly woman, dark-haired, round-faced, seemingly mature. No Gucci sunglasses. No fake tan. In Rafa's camp, his parents. Rafa is only 22. Dad is his coach. Mum is his lover.

Every bit of this contest screamed archetype. And every spectator tuned into those archetypes. They are written in our biology. They are pre-verbal essences. In the clenched silence, as Rafa prepared to serve in the final game, a lone female voice cried, 'I love you, Rafa.'

And Rafa won. He clambered up to the stands to hug his mum and dad. Both Roger and Rafa were interviewed. Both were nice. Both said the right thing. The drama had dissolved. It was only ever a play. And the crowd went home, smiling at it, with something affirmed, something old and wordless.

Experts say

O *Sunday Star-Times*, I prayed, as I often do, please tell me how bad things are, especially with regard to mortgagee sales. And don't bury the article on page 17 among the ads for phone sex and sun-drenched indoor outdoor living in Taupo. Stick it on the front page, please, under a banner headline so I shall know the worst. A horror known, however dreadful, is better than a horror imagined. And last weekend the *Sunday Star-Times*, as it often does, answered my prayer.

'New data has revealed,' the article began, and I knew at once that I was in for a tough read. Data are true things, impossible to ignore or to dispute. (They are also plural things and require a plural verb, but when the data are this bad, grammar can go hang.)

'New data has revealed the extent of the mortgagee-sale wave now sweeping New Zealand.'

Nice of the writer to soften the blow, but who could miss the import of her words? Mere waves don't sweep across land. Only tsunamis do. And I pictured the tsunami of mortgagee sales crossing the country at the speed of a trotting horse, trillions of tons of misery thumping into the mountains, then seething back to the sea in a frothing nightmare of destruction. The few survivors would be left in a world of dead sheep, ruined land and shoals of gasping flapping soon-to-die householders.

'Oh, tell me those data,' I begged. 'I need details.' The

second paragraph obliged. In January 2009 the tsunami of mortgagee sales across New Zealand numbered 150.

But how bad was that? Why not, I thought, compare January 2009 with January 2007 when the country was economically buoyant, thereby supplying the most terrifying possible contrast? The writer read my thoughts. Mortgagee sales in January 2007 had numbered only 28.

In other words there had been a five-fold increase over 2007 — or rather a 'whopping five-fold increase'.

'Oh gosh,' I said, 'but won't you tell me what this whopping five-fold increase, as opposed to those insignificant five-fold increases one comes across, means for you and me, the terrified burghers of this beleaguered land?'

Never underestimate the modesty of the journalists at the *Sunday Star-Times*. They do not scaremonger in order to sell papers and neither do they interpret. They deal only in hard data. Should interpretation be required, they consult. And whom do they consult? They consult experts.

'Experts say,' began paragraph three, and my heart went boom bang a bang.

For if experts say anything, it is true. There's no need to name the experts, or to identify the source of their expertise. When the tsunami comes at the speed of a trotting horse you don't hang round asking pernickety questions about the nature of expertise. You run.

'Experts say the crisis is starting to hit average Kiwi families.'

In other words, the tsunami was bearing down on average you and average me and the average girl next door. I could hear the clip of its hooves.

The conclusion was inescapable. Below-average families

had already been flattened. One hundred and fifty mortgagee sales a month had done for the lot of them. They and their houses were toast, sodden tsunamied toast. And now the tsunami had trotted up the income scale and we, the average, the citizens of the middle, were now in its path. To be safe you had to be above-average. And for how long would even the above-average be safe? Once the average families had been swallowed by the merciless mortgagee waters, then the above-average would become the average. And this was not scaremongering. This was data. This was what the experts say. And experts know.

What to do? Run, obviously. But where to? Nowhere is immune. Mortgagee sales in Wellington, for example, the capital of the nation, the seat of an impotent government, soared from five in January 2008 to no fewer than seven in January 2009. That's a 40 per cent rise.

Maybe things are better beyond the mountains in the rural haven of the Manawatu? No, they're worse. In the Manawatu the increase in mortgagee sales was 300 terrifying per cent. A single mortgagee sale there in January 2008 had rocketed to four in January 2009.

Where then should the terrified average Kiwi family go? To the coast perhaps?

No, no and no again. The data tell us that Taranaki experienced an increase in mortgagee sales so proportionally vast that it cannot be measured, an infinite increase. From no mortgagee sales at all in January 2008 the number soared in January 2009 to one. Is nowhere safe? No, nowhere is safe. We are doomed. Experts say so. Thank you, *Sunday Star-Times*.

Coming to get you

'Mummy.'

'Yes darling, what is it? Though may I just say before I attend to your childish question how lovely it is to hear your innocent voice piping from the multiply-buckled safety seat in the back of the SUV that I use for the kindergarten run every morning and afternoon. And may I add, for the purpose of establishing the scene a little more clearly in the reader's mind, how sweet it is to be driving you along Ferry Road in the south of Christchurch this winter's afternoon, though the name of the particular road is unimportant since Ferry Road is representative, I suspect, of any suburban thoroughfare in that it is flanked by shops and numerous . . .'

'Billboards, Mummy.'

'Oh, what a clever girl you are. And how fitting that one of your first clearly enunciated words should be "billboards" since you have been born into a society of unprecedented commercial persuasiveness, of which billboards form only a part. In your early years, my little bundle of joy, you will be addressed by advertisers and governmental agencies through numerous media, some overt, some insidious, but all of them trying to plant seeds in your untroubled skull, seeds that will sprout into wants, and wants that will sprout into verbal wheedling aimed at me, your harassed mummy, who loves you more than she loves life herself and who will be easily persuaded to wave her credit card and buy you anything you want, partly from a wish to please you and partly from a need to shut you up. So what is it, my pretty one?'

'Mummy, do you or someone close to you have a gambling problem?'

'Does, darling, does. You really must grasp the anachronistic variation of the auxiliary verb in the third person. "Do you or *does* someone close to you have a gambling problem?"'

'But that's what it said on the billboard, Mummy.'

'Oh darling, hallelujah, you can read already. All that Mozart I played to you in the womb must be paying off. I give thanks for the *Encyclopaedia of Modern Birthing*. But above all, I give thanks for you, Cassiopeia, my only child, my precious darling, whom, in accordance with the middle-class zeitgeist, I have saddled with a name so distinctive that I am confident you share it with no one at all. You're a prodigy. The Centre for Gifted Children, here we come!'

'But do you, or does someone close to you, have a gambling problem, Mummy? I'm worried, Mummy. The picture of the woman on the gambling helpline billboard looked just like you when you are waiting for Daddy to come home from the . . . Oh no, Mummy, no, no, no, help, no, I am inarticulately screaming with horror.'

'What is it, my darling, my honeypie, my distillation of all sweet things? What's upsetting you? Tell Mummy, even as she screeches to a halt in the outside lane to attend to your appalling distress.'

'It's the intersection up ahead, Mummy, the horrid

intersection. Please don't go to the intersection, Mummy. You may make a bad call at the intersection and it says on the billboard over there that bad calls can be deadly. We could be deadlied. Oh, please don't go to the intersection, Mummy, or I'll scream and I'll . . .'

'There, there, darling, don't you worry your little . . .'

'Oh golly, look up there, Mummy. Smoking kills. And there's a picture of, of, oh, it's too horrid. Quick, call the quitline now.'

'But I don't smoke, darling.'

'Oh Mummy, please call the quitline, please, just for me, your little Cassiopeia who is becoming generically frightened of all the nasties out there and would be begging you on bended knee if it weren't for the restrictions of this multiply-buckled safety seat. Please, Mummy, please.'

'Very well, my sweetness, read me the number off the billboard and I'll dial it on my funky pink BlackBerry which is both an essential technological accessory and, remarkably, a cellphone.'

'*No*! Mummy, *no*, *no*, *no*. Using your phone when driving is deadly too. It says so on the billboard. Oh Mummy, I want to go home.'

'Home it is then, darling.'

'*Stop*! I'm approaching inarticulate screaming once again. You haven't cleaned the windscreen.'

'Why should I clean the windscreen, my sweetest?'

'Sunstrike, Mummy. The billboard up there says sunstrike can kill. Did Grandpa get sunstrike, Mummy?'

'No dear, Grandpa just died of old age at 104 having spent his years smoking his way through intersections without ever cleaning his windscreen. How he lived that long I'll never know.'

'Oh Mummy, I'm so frightened. It's such a scary world. When we get home can we huddle under the bed and stay there trembling for approximately the next 80 years?'

'Of course, my sweetness. But you do know what's under the bed, don't you? Can you spell paedophile?'

Lovefruit

Not once in my life, not once, have I bought broccoli at the supermarket. I acknowledge that the stuff is just about edible if disguised by a pint of cheese sauce, but so is a running shoe. So can you explain why, when I saw a punnet of six broccoli seedlings at The Warehouse for $3.99, I bought them? No, neither can I. This gardening business is mysterious.

I paid $3.99 for a strawberry plant as well, but that was less mysterious. I like strawberries. And the plant already had an embryonic strawberry attached. It was green and hard as a nut, but it sang a song of summer joy. For the drive home I put the broccoli in the boot to take its chances, but I nursed the infant strawberry in my lap.

Back home I rammed the broccoli seedlings into their bed any old which way, but I planted the strawberry with a mother's loving care and laid the head of the infant berry as gently as a dove on a manger of dried pine needles. This strawberry would know it was loved. I would nurse it, cradle it, sing to it, praise it, feed and water it, and watch it grow up. Whereupon, and this is perhaps when the batteries run down on the mother and child metaphor, I would eat it.

The broccoli obeyed the first mysterious law of gardening, which is that anything you don't much care for flourishes. It rapidly sprouted leaves the size and colour of battleships. But then the battleships developed mysterious holes.

'Caterpillars,' said Helen authoritatively down the phone, 'cabbage white caterpillars.'

'But broccoli isn't cabbage,' I said.

'Brassicas,' she said.

'Bless you,' I said.

'No,' she said, 'brassicas. The family of vegetables that cabbage whites love and children don't. You know, cabbages, broccoli, sprouts.'

'Wise things, children,' I said. But I knew she was right. I'd seen the cabbage whites inspecting my garden. Thanks to Helen I now knew that rather than being fluttery and decorative, they were a sort of B52 squadron seeking brassicas to bomb. But I still couldn't see how they survived. They fly like aeronautical drunks. Incapable of travelling in a straight line they go, as Robert Graves put it, 'by guess and God and hopelessness'. How do they cope with even the slightest breeze? With their huge frail sails slung either side of a maggot of ballast, they look about as airworthy as those winged machines that men used to strap themselves into in the late 19th century so as to run flapping down a pier and fall immediately into the sea. Why, when a breeze picks up, don't butterflies just slam into walls and fall in a twitching heap of wings and eggs? Mystery piled on mystery.

'Derris dust,' said Helen interrupting my lucubrations. 'Derris dust'll get the buggers.' Helen's saintly exterior masks a Dr Crippen heart.

At Mitre 10 a shaker of derris dust cost me $12.99. I had now spent $16.98 on some infant vegetables that might need who knew how many other expensive medical interventions before attaining edible adulthood, and that I then wouldn't eat.

But at least my strawberry was prospering. Every morning on the way up the hill with the dog I inspected it, watching it swell and go from green to speckled white to its first pink flush. And every morning I would puff and plump its pine needle pillow and with solicitous caution rotate the berry a fraction on its stem to ensure an all-over tan.

Then another mystery. For years my couple of acres have been a rose-free zone. But within weeks of my planting a single Margaret Merril, greenfly found it. How? Had they been lurking all this while? Or did Greenfly HQ send regular reconnaissance missions over my land just in case. I didn't know and don't care.

Derris dust seemed to have little effect on them. So every morning on the way back down from my strawberry I now just smear them to death between finger and thumb. I have even tried, but so far without success, to encourage the dog to lick my fingers afterwards in the hope that he'll gain a taste for the little critters.

But it is summer and I'm a gardener, so the bright side is where I look. And yesterday dawned bright as a diamond. Up the hill went the dog and I and my single strawberry was visible from 5 metres. It was red as a ruby. To see it was to salivate.

'Look at that,' I said to the dog. 'After a couple of months of gardening and who knows how many hundred dollars here, at last, on this glorious morning, is the first fruit of our labours and my wallet.' The dog sniffed the berry, then bit off the pointy end. I ate what was left.

Naomi's good

Naomi Campbell, the talented supermodel, has apologised for assaulting two police officers on a British Airways plane. But she has refused to apologise to the airline. I am uncertain how one goes about apologising to an airline — 'Dear British Airways,' I suppose, 'I'm frightfully sorry' — but it doesn't matter because Naomi won't do it. She said that someone on the plane had called her a racial name, to wit 'a golliwog supermodel', and that someone wasn't a passenger. Because she'd been called a golliwog supermodel she felt justified in shouting abuse at the plane's captain, who had not called her a golliwog supermodel. She also insisted that some missing luggage of hers be found by someone who had also not called her a golliwog supermodel, she caused the plane to be delayed, along with all its passengers, none of whom, as she has explicitly stated, had called her a golliwog supermodel, and she allegedly spat at one of the police officers, who hadn't called her a golliwog supermodel either.

The supermodelling world has reacted swiftly and variously to the performance.

'Naomi's good,' said a spokesperson for Tall and Vacuous Inc., the supermodelling agency. 'It's a tough world out there for supermodels and few people appreciate quite how tough. Consider the requirements of the job. You have to be freakishly tall and thin. When working you have to sit still while people take you to exotic locations, you have to stand still while people pin clothes on you and then you have to lie down while people take photographs of you. Sometimes you have to parade along a catwalk in a style that no human frame manages naturally. It takes a pretty special person to cope with all that. Admittedly you are allowed to jump around and holler when you see the number of zeroes that have landed in your bank account, but even then you have to ensure that the curtains are drawn in case paparazzi are stationed on ladders outside your Malibu apartment. Or your London mansion. Or your chalet in Cannes.'

'Naomi's good,' said Ron Stutter, agent for many of the leading supermodels. 'She's got star quality. But it's tough out there. Like any supermodel she works in a post-verbal environment. Language is the sister of thought and thought is the wicked stepfather of the fashion business. When anyone puts what they're doing into words the whole industry collapses in on itself. Not being allowed to speak also makes it difficult to find your way into the headlines with the requisite frequency. So a supermodel has to use her precious free time to do her own publicity. The poor dear is never off duty. A few years ago Naomi pulled a cracking stunt, biffing a cellphone at her maid ostensibly over a lost pair of jeans. The ensuing court case meant I was able to pin several unprecedented zeroes onto her invoices, but ideas that good don't come along every day. I think she's done herself proud here.'

'Naomi's good,' said Judy Adverb, the supermodel gossip columnist. 'But she's still got work to do if she wants to stack up with the legends. The yardstick for this sort of outburst was that true queen of the catwalk, Bulimia Beckons. What old Bully didn't know about pulling a stunt wasn't worth knowing. Fingernails an inch long and always ready to sink them into the scrotum of any reporter who came within ten feet of her. The tabloids loved it. Remember those coke-binges? And the attempted murder rap on the Japanese doorman who didn't bow low enough? And what about that time she hanged her chihuahua for pissing on her otter-fur stole? Oh, that girl knew the business inside out. Naomi's still got a ways to go before she makes the truly top flight.'

'Naomi's good,' said Salman Pierce, counsellor, shrink and substance-peddler to most of the top supermodels. 'Her PSI index is off the scale — oh sorry, jargon. Preposterous Self-Importance — and she's getting there with both the brittle-psyche routine and the ungovernable temper. But she does need to work on her sense of fatuity. She has yet to fully grasp the inane nature of her job. And when she comes to grips with ephemerality, then watch out. I've introduced her to several of the absurdist playwrights but she tends to hold the books upside down, and she lost her copy of Sartre's *Huis-clos* when she threw it at a flunky in Madagascar who failed to recognise her. I'm going to try her with Andrew Marvell this week:

> But at my back I always hear
> Time's winged chariot hurrying near,
> And yonder all before us lie
> Deserts of vast eternity.

I'm not certain of holding her attention but if I can just squeeze those four lines in that busy professional skull of hers, then we'll see a proper tantrum. Naomi's good.'

On buying a jogger

So you're thinking of getting a jogger as a pet. Well, it's up to you, of course, but my advice is simple. Don't.

Let me say at the outset that a jogger should not be confused with a runner. A runner is easily identified. Its thighs begin at its shoulders, and its whole frame is built like the runner bean from which it derived its name.

Runners can be found in all parts of the globe but are most common in Africa where they can be picked up quite cheaply. The going price is an athletic scholarship to a western university. So acquire a runner by all means. It may even add lustre to your nation by winning athletic medals, thereby suggesting that its new compatriots are not all slobs.

But a runner is not a jogger. A runner runs because it must. A jogger jogs only through force of will. A jogger does not win medals nor is it a jewel in the crown of its adopted home. A jogger is a burden. That may seem harsh, but I am not here to spare feelings. I am here to save you from a decision you will regret.

A jogger is for life. And some of them live a very long time. So before you buy, try picturing that cute young jogger 40 years down the track, scrawny as an ancient fowl, but still pulling on a stained singlet and health-hazard training shoes in your kitchen. Ignore that image and the old saw, 'Act in haste; repent at leisure', will cut you in half.

Some of you, nevertheless, and in defiance of all warnings,

will go ahead and acquire one. If you do, you should mark your ownership. An identity disc can be attached to the creature's collar, but my preference is for branding. It is cheap, permanent and entirely painless so long as you wear asbestos gloves. The greatest advantage, however, is that the brand can be applied to a discreet part of the anatomy so when your jogger is at large it is not immediately obvious who owns it.

The law does not yet require you to neuter your jogger, but common sense does. You just don't want them reproducing. DIY neutering kits are available from all good pet shops.

Before taking a jogger home, be sure to have it checked out by a competent physician. Almost every jogger is psychologically mutilated and riddled with paradox. Indeed paradox in joggers is endemic and to some degree incurable. The jogger's motivation is to live longer. It wants to live longer so as to enjoy more life. But in order to enjoy more life it engages in an activity that it clearly loathes. To date no explanation of this paradox has been found, let alone a cure.

You will be abused for owning a jogger. Over recent years Joe Public has become increasingly intolerant of anything he perceives as an infringement of his rights. I don't pretend it's admirable but you will be told to put your jogger on a leash, and to keep it away from public places. And to some degree the public's attitude is understandable. The presence of a jogger is not an aesthetic embellishment to the environment, especially if you allow it to wear those cut-away shorts that reveal thighs to waist level.

Jogging is a selfish condition and selfishness is unpleasant to live with. If you want affection, get a dog. But as it happens, one of the few advantages of owning a jogger is that it will bring you into regular and delightful communion with dogs.

Dogs are born to run and will often mistake a jogger for a fellow runner. They will run alongside it and leap up to invite it to join their joyful games. Your monomaniac jogger is unlikely to welcome the invitation and friction may ensue, for which you are entirely responsible.

To give you some idea of what you are letting myself in for, let me tell you what happened to me this morning. Some reprobate had allowed his jogger to trespass on a dog beach. Worse still the jogger was wearing an iPod. A jogger is perpetually half-blinded by sweat and self-hatred, so it is thoughtless cruelty to allow it to deafen itself as well. It becomes a threat to traffic and itself.

My dog spotted the jogger from afar. Motivated partly by a desire to play, but also, I suspect, by an altruistic wish to save the jogger from its self-centred misery, my dog bounded after it. The jogger, of course, didn't hear it coming. The dog leapt and planted playful paws on the jogger's back. I have rarely heard a louder squeal. Then the jogger tripped. When I eventually reached the scene, the jogger was on its back and the dog was trying to lick its face. Astonishingly, the jogger was furious. It lashed out at both me and the dog. Its owner was nowhere to be seen. Hiding behind a tree, I suspect. And if you ignore my counsel you could be that owner.

Eventually, I hope and trust, the authorities will institute a licensing system to encourage responsible jogger ownership, but until that day I would frankly advise you to keep well away from the whole grim business.

The reality is

The world's most wanted man has appeared on trial in The Hague. Remarkably he had been hiding for years in his native capital city. Even more remarkably he had deceived the authorities by masquerading as a statesman.

The accused entered court in a treble-breasted suit by Smarm Bros.

'Are you,' said the judge, 'Mr Winston Petersich?'

'Don't try that on me, you scumbag journalist disguised as a judge,' said the accused. 'The reality is I know your sort. I didn't come down in the last shower.'

'Would you mind answering the question?' said the judge, then paused for two and a half days to allow the applause from New Zealand to die down.

'Yes,' said the accused. The court gasped. 'I would mind answering the question. The reality is I didn't get where I am today by answering questions. When faced with a question it is my unfailing method to resort to accusation and incoherence.'

'Mr Petersich,' said the judge. 'In the interests of compressing this trial into an 800-word newspaper column I have decided to drop the host of minor charges, to wit, hypocrisy, obfuscation, self-interest, ineffectuality, overweening vanity, inciting racial prejudice for the purposes of reburying your snout troughwise, and beginning every second sentence with "the reality is" regardless of its lack of any relevance to reality. I am laying only the one charge.

'Mr Petersich, you stand accused of having made the following statement in a language yet to be identified but bearing superficial resemblance to English: "New Zealand has just experienced a media ego-explosion. It works like a neutron bomb — the egos remain intact but the truth is ignored and the fact that I am back now with not one question with respect to the matters raised when I was away tells you volumes." How do you plead?'

'Plead,' exclaimed the accused, 'you expect me to plead? The reality is when my friend Condoleezza, who loves nothing more than to be photographed with me, gets to hear about . . .'

'Silence!' bellowed the judge, then paused for a month to allow the applause from New Zealand to die down. 'We are already halfway through the column and nothing of substance has been said. That may seem normal to you but to me it does not. Call the first imaginary expert witness.'

A huge man shambled into the witness box clutching a glass of aquavit. In response to the judge's questioning he acknowledged that he was Horst Bangmeister, a Norwegian expert on nuclear armaments, and that he had studied the words that the accused was charged with having spoken.

'And what scientific conclusions did you draw?'

'You are a joke making?' said the giant Norwegian. 'The speaker of these words incontrovertibly either ignorant or bonkers and probably both is.'

'Is it legitimate,' asked the judge, 'to compare the explosion of a neutron bomb to media egos, and if so would those egos remain intact after the explosion while simultaneously ignoring the truth?'

'Your question is no sense whatsoever making,' said Mr Bangmeister, taking a large swig of aquavit. 'The active ingredient of a neutron bomb is tritium, a radioactive isotope with a half-life of 12.3 years. When the bomb explodes the tritium disintegrates, releasing a prodigious quantity of neutrons. In nuclear fission bombs these neutrons are absorbed. In a neutron bomb they are deliberately emitted. The result is a slight loss of explosive force but a huge gain in radiation.'

'Your English syntax seems to have improved markedly, Mr Bangmeister.'

'I am from Wikipedia more or less directly quoting,' said Horst.

'In your opinion, Mr Bangmeister, does the speaker have any notion of how a neutron bomb works?'

'His simile from any semblance of coherence a very long way has wandered. You do not a nuclear expert but a language expert require. I am to my beloved fjords cornily returning,' and so saying Mr Bangmeister left the court, his verbs behind him dragging.

'In that case,' said the judge, 'I summon the 250-year-old corpse of Dr Samuel Johnson, compiler of the first dictionary of the English language. Dr Johnson, have you studied the words allegedly spoken by the accused?'

'I have. I am unable to judge the opening figure of speech since I died before the neutron was discovered. But I am competent to judge the second half of the statement.'

'And?'

'It looks like language but closer inspection reveals it to be merely noise. It resembles the combative gibbering of a chimpanzee.'

'I see,' said the judge. 'On that basis, do you have any general observation to make concerning the linguistic or public behaviour of Mr Petersich, perhaps in epigrammatic form, and maybe drawn from the *Oxford Book of Quotations* in which you figure so prominently?'

'Yes. Stubborn audacity is the last refuge of guilt.'

'The reality is,' began the defendant from the dock, but it was too late. The dead Dr Johnson had completed the 800-word requirement rather nicely.

Nuts

Follow me. Up past the pumpkin with its single fruit that I plan to pluck soon. It's the size of a balled fist. I'll harden it off in the sun that we don't seem to have any more and then store it in a dark place to keep the wolf from the door during the cruel months of winter. Not that I get many wolves at the door because my steep drive deters them. But it doesn't deter the Jehovah's Witnesses whose devotion to nonsense keeps them climbing up up up to the heaven of my house. I'd prefer wolves.

My dog wouldn't. He's a saint, and a kinder judge of people than Jehovah. According to my dog, if you're human you are good and you deserve a game. The game's called Leap, Scrabble, Whimper with Love, and Leap Some More. If the other player is holding a stack of religious pamphlets crammed with preposterous sentiments, the aim of the game, at which my dog is world champion, is to dislodge those pamphlets. Very few of the Witnesses seem to have grasped the rules. Their pamphlets scatter with the breeze and float away to the paddock where the goats eat them with no noticeable ill effects, except to the pamphlets, which emerge some hours later in a form befitting their content. Oh, it's a mad world we inhabit.

But anyway, in the absence of wolves, Witnesses and lunacy, join me and my dog up the hill. We're going farming. The very best form of farming. Through the gate we pass into the paddock that is even steeper than the drive. Ignore the burn in your thighs. Don't dally under the pine trees with their deep beds of dried needles, so cool and good in the high summer that's gone. We're climbing to a better place, the ridge where the land levels out a bit. It's a Golgotha of dogs. Two dogs are buried there, Jessie and Baz, under cairns of stones. The cairns are sinking as the dogs rot. A little clay plaque stands beside each cairn. Present dog, Blue, the lover of Witnesses, will probably rot here too one day, not that he knows it and not that he'd care if he did. He's too busy with joy. It's a good sane world he inhabits.

I'd like to be dug in here too, but I bet the pestilential authorities won't allow it. I'll be sent to ground consecrated by bishops or similar witch doctors, none of them a jot wiser than the Witnesses, just less committed to climbing. Bugger them. Bugger the lot of them. Up here in dog Golgotha you can shout such emphatic wisdom to the world and there's no one to listen but the dogs who don't care. It's good up here.

Behind the cairns a fence to keep the goats off. And behind the fence a tree, a walnut tree. Keep really quiet and you can hear it groaning. Groaning under its burden of nuts, an image that tempts me to a comparison that would upset the Witnesses.

I've done nothing to this tree except fence it to keep the goats off and give it a couple of dog corpses to feast on. Yet it has responded with bounty, a monstrous uncountable profusion of nuts.

The dog snuffles round the remains of his predecessors. No reverence there. Sing heigh ho, there's sense in the life of the senses, and none in the life of the mind. And while he snuffles and fossicks and scrapes at a rabbit scrape and scans the horizon for believers to molest with love, you and I are going nutting.

Walnuts look like unripe golf balls, all green and smooth and round and throwable, until the earth tilts and the days shorten and the smooth green casing withers and splits to reveal, held lightly in its splayed and ruined fingers, a nut. A little brown nut like a reptilian brain. The nut hangs there till the wind or a man shakes it, then down it tumbles, rattling lightly through the branches to be eaten by possums, rats or decay.

But we'll pre-empt that tumble. Clamber with me into the branches, monkeys regressing, cumbersome and clumsy, dressed in Chinese cotton rather than fur, and carrying a plastic bag from Woolworths. Into that bag we drop nuts. Our fingers turn nicotine brown with the juices.

Down from the tree we swing like lumpen gibbons, laden with booty, landing on dog graves. Down the hill singing, the living dog prancing with the pleasure of everything, back through the gate and past the pumpkin that will get us through winter and down to the house where we'll feast on nuts. Nuts to the lot of them. Nuts to everything. Nuts.

Bye-bye, little nothing

'Ladies and gentlemen, brothers and sisters in grammar,' said the preacher, 'we are gathered here together to mourn a passing. The passing was not unexpected. We had all known it would come. Indeed in those long final years some of us wished that it would come sooner than it did. For they were sorry years. Years of neglect and abuse. Years of increasing irrelevance. But now at last the end is here.

'What each of us is feeling at this moment is private to each of us. But I would ask you all to bow your heads and remember the long, strange and instructive life of our friend the little apostrophe.'

The mourners chins drop to their chests as one, then lift again. Desperate eyes flick around the graveyard, seeking. Awareness dawns simultaneously on every face. They will not find what they seek. The apostrophe is gone. Mourners chins are mourners chins, for now and for ever after, amen. The chins sink. There is sniffling, gulps, then a long slow silence.

In the silence a breeze rises, stirs the dead leaves that lie about the grave like shrivelled paper, then rustles the preachers robe. Yea verily, the preachers robe. The mourners look up. Some manage to smile, weakly.

'Thank you,' says the preacher. He too is smiling. 'I have decided on this unique occasion to dispense with ceremony. For one thing I am unsure whether the apostrophe was a piece of punctuation or a diacritical mark and the funeral liturgy is different for each. But, more significantly, I believe that the best way to honour our late friend is with silence. For it was in silence that the apostrophe spent its days. It was visible but it had no voice. In conversation one did not know whether it was there or not, though rather often, I must admit, one suspected not. But your presence here today and your deep silence has done it proud. If any of you should now wish to speak, the floor is yours.'

A pause, then up to the head of the tiny grave limps a broken man in duffle coat and satchel. 'I taught,' he said. 'I fought hard for our friend. I spent years in its service. I leaked red ink like blood. But the battle is done now and lost, and I speak only to forgive.

'All of us here believe we know the murderer. The name hangs in the air unspoken. That name is the Birmingham City Council. For it was the Birmingham City Council that banished the apostrophe, that decreed it should never again be used in council sign-writing. Thus they plunged the fatal dagger in our old friends — oh, the grief of it — heart. But listen to me, good people. The council did not forge the steel of that dagger or fashion the blade. It merely delivered the blow. Fault lies, if fault there is, in public ignorance born of indolence. So let us not lay blame. Let us mourn and move on. May the apostrophe rest in peace. I shall join it soon. We will lie together. For, to put it as simply as I can, I loved it. I have spoken and I am done.' As the old man turned to shuffle alone from the graveyard even the leaves ceased their rustling.

'Good riddance.' The voice was jaunty, strong. All faces turned to the speaker. He wore a sharp suit and a fat grin.

'Good riddance to bad rubbish. The apostrophe was a snobs (sic) sick delight and I have come here today, to this sorry gathering on Pedants (sic and hallelujah) Green, to dance on its grave. Watch me, you stick-in-the-muds. Watch me, you anachronisms. Watch the Death Jig of the Apostrophe, or rather (sic and hallelujah) the Apostrophes Death Jig.'

So saying he leapt onto the little hummock of freshly turned soil and jigged, kicking up his merry knees till the sweat gleamed on his face. The mourners stood and stared. Whatever outrage they may have felt, they remained as silent and as formal as the apostrophe itself.

The man ceased his jig. He put his hands to his suited knees to recover his breath. Then he hauled himself upright once more and he spoke. 'People, I ask you, what good did the apostrophe ever do? Did it clarify? Did it help? No, ladies and gentlemen, it did not. Its only function was to divide man from man. It split the world into those who could use it and those who could not. And each despised the other.

'Shakespeare knew nothing of the apostrophe, ladies and gentlemen, and Chaucer less. It discouraged children and it baffled greengrocers. It was the grammatical equivalent of a Masonic handshake. It perpetuated a smug élite who sneered at the mob. I delight in its demise. May it rot in hell.'

He stopped and he beamed. The mourners turned as one. They turned in silence and departed, each making his way in a diminished world.

Investigating booze

Its conclusions were as inevitable as death. You and I could have reached them in a fifth of the time at a tenth of the price, but that is neither here nor there because you and I somehow never get jobs like this. The people who get jobs like this are the people who get jobs like this.

I have often wondered about the gravy train that delivers these jobs. How does it decide which stations to call at? I've been waiting on the platform for years, peering hopefully down the line, watching the shimmering rails narrow with distance, yet never hearing those rails hum with the approach of gravy-bearing carriages. And now it's too late. Ah well, it's probably for the best. Gravy goes well with flesh but poorly with soul.

The job in question was to investigate booze. See what I mean? You and I have been diligently investigating the stuff for years, but it crossed nobody's mind to consult our expertise. Oh no, the job went to the usual collection of besuited officials and ex-prime ministers and other suckers from the Treasury teat.

They were required to investigate booze and make recommendations to the government. Astonishingly it took them several months. Right now, without thought, I've got a string of recommendations about booze with which no one could find fault: always make sure there's some around; apply several glasses immediately to visiting relatives; never pay more than $10 for a bottle of wine, because after the first three glasses they all taste the same, and so on until bedtime.

The source of such wisdom is that undervalued stalwart, experience. Experience presents no statistics. Experience offers no facts. It simply depends on the reductive capacity of the humming human brain, which accepts sensory data over the years and reduces it by some strange and beautiful composting process to nuggets of truth. But nuggets of truth count for nothing on commissions of inquiry. Commissions want what they call hard facts, and hard facts have the same relation to truth as the instructions for opening a can of sardines have to King Lear.

But anyway, the commission assembled, congratulated itself on its own appointment, bought a lot of stationery, a brace of secretaries and a photocopier the size of a small car, and then adjourned for a well-lubricated lunch of gravy. Several months of lunches later it drew its conclusions.

All of which were as predictable as tertiary syphilis: that booze is bad; that booze causes a trillion dollars of expense to the public coffers a year; that the tax on booze brings in a lot less than a trillion; and that therefore, *therefore*, mind you, the excise tax on booze should be raised prodigiously, and the permitted level of booze on the breath of car drivers should be reduced to so minimal a level that driving past a grog shop with the window down puts them in danger of being placed in the public stocks and pelted by the mob with bottles of sports water.

And you can't argue with any of that, can you? You may want to, you may feel in the gut that there's something wrong there, but this is incontrovertible factual and financial stuff and there is simply no disputing incontrovertible factual and financial stuff, nor the moral and legal conclusions that follow from it with the inevitability of night following day.

Well, I shall argue. I shall dispute. I, who, in 35 or more years of knocking back the booze, have hurt nobody excluding myself, run over nobody including myself, done damage to nothing except a real estate For Sale sign (about which I feel no guilt whatsoever, none, do you hear me?) and have laughed one hell of a lot more and been one hell of a lot happier than I would have been if I'd never touched a drop.

Sad? Of course it's sad. It's a sad world. The burden of consciousness is too great a burden for us feeble beasts. And the complexities of urban society are too great for us feeble beasts. And the paradox of being mortal creatures with a notion of immortality is too great for us feeble beasts. So we drink.

Go now, this evening, and stand outside a bar. Go on. Listen to the pleasure, the happiness, the release. Social workers, digger drivers, lecturers, undertakers, agronomists, accountants, all, for once, because of booze, telling the truth and laughing.

Yes, I've known hopeless addicts and intolerable bores and inexcusable fighters and habitual vandals, for all of whom booze is a bad, bad thing. And yes, I've seen streets awash with vomit and I've seen what the police have to deal with and I've seen misery. But I have also seen joy, radiant joy, good joy, release from a burden. And that joy, that release, that incontrovertible good, didn't make it into the hard facts of the commission of inquiry. It was omitted. And you and I, the good drinkers who are in the huge majority, shall in consequence be bullied and fleeced.

Meant for someone else

Love, goes the song, love changes everything, da da dum dum, da da dum.

And a very nice song it is too, but it would make more sense if you replaced the word love with glasses. Indeed there comes a time in life when glasses make more sense than love in any song: 'All you need is glasses', 'I thought glasses were only true in fairy tales/Meant for someone else but not for me'. The rhythm may be shot, but the truth rings out like a bell.

Glasses change the way you see the world. Glasses change the way others see you. Glasses change the way you see yourself.

Children with glasses suffer at school. Or at least they did at my school. They began from a position of perceived weakness. If a boy with glasses wanted to get into the football team he had to be twice as good as a boy without glasses. He wasn't. Partly because he had to take the glasses off in order to play, which meant that he was trying to catch or kick a blur. And partly because he was simply a boy with glasses, which meant that he was heading for a whizzbang career as a librarian.

Yes I know, I know, that's simplistic and prejudicial. But it's how children think. They go from observation to judgment with the unswerving immediacy of a bullet. Glasses equals nerd. Children behave like a flock of pigeons who all decide simultaneously to descend on a single weak or injured pigeon. One moment they're contentedly brooping and bobbing their heads, the next there's a frenzy of feathered assault that ends as suddenly as it began, with every pigeon bar one returning to brooping and head bobbing. The one has been pecked to death.

I saw exactly that happen in Sloane Square in London once and I immediately thought of school. In particular I thought of Errol, who was the son of a maths teacher and was inevitably therefore preceded everywhere he went by about a kilo of optical glass. He was just as inevitably followed by a gang of unpleasant laser-eyed tykes whose ambition was to snatch the glasses from Errol's nose and place them somewhere he couldn't reach, assuming, that is, he was capable of seeing his glasses without his glasses on, which he wasn't. I wonder which library he's in now. Or which home.

'Men seldom make passes,' said Dorothy Parker, who as far as I can tell spent her entire life knocking up epigrams, which would have made her a momentarily sparkling conversationalist about once a week and a mumbling distracted bore the rest of the time, 'at girls who wear glasses.' The porn industry has heroically spent years trying to eradicate this prejudice by depicting bespectacled librarians as only too keen to let down their hair, remove their glasses and sizzle. But it hasn't worked.

Two years ago I needed glasses to read the phone book. Now I need glasses to read anything. And I discovered yesterday that if I want to read the instructions on a packet of Maggi Chicken Cacciatore food powder additive, even glasses aren't enough. I had to hold the packet under a bright light and squint. I tried putting a pair of glasses in front of the glasses I was already wearing but for some reason of School Cert. physics that I was too busy bullying Errol to pay attention to, it didn't work.

For the last 20 odd years whenever I've stared into the mirror I've somehow been able to overlook the gleaming skull, the abuse-battered teeth, the ravines in the flesh, and have beheld the twinkling cherub of youth grinning back at me from the ruins. But glasses are one piece of evidence too many. The case for the defence collapses like a soufflé. I'm done for.

For parsimonious reasons I buy hobby glasses for 10 bucks from The Warehouse. My hobby is pretending to myself that they are only a temporary measure and that soon my eyes will return to the falcon acuity of youth. They won't. They're shot. That's it.

Almost as bad is that glasses have become an extra chunk of paraphernalia that I have to remember to take with me. Last week I gave a speech to some lawyers. The room was candle-lit dinner darkish. As I told an introductory one-liner I flattened my speech notes on the lectern, glanced down and beheld the phone book in Arabic. I patted my pocket for glasses. They weren't there. It wasn't a good moment.

When I leave the house I automatically check that I've got wallet and smokes. But I still have to make a conscious decision to check I've got glasses. That requires memory. And has anyone else ever noticed the cruel correlation between failing eyesight and failing memory? As the old song puts it, da da dum dum, da da dum.

By any other name

Naming a child is tricky and some parents get it wrong. I went to primary school with S. Tinker and to secondary school with S. Melling. I taught three John Thomases and a boy called Fallik. Near my rooms at university there was a medical practice run by Dr G. Roper. It had a brass name plate on the door. I longed to steal it. But every night I got drunk enough I found that someone had beaten me to it.

These names weren't meant to be funny, but on television this week I saw a list of real names that were. My favourite was Number Sixteen Bus Shelter. It conjured a scene. That scene starred a couple who met at a party and had each drunk enough to find the other beautiful. They left together. I pictured rain and a bus that didn't arrive, street lights glistening on the wet road, no one about but them, conversation sinking to silence, a cuddle, a fumble, awkward adjustments of posture, rising heartbeats and the roaring arrival of the bus of brief happiness. Then the long trudge home. But at least the couple did the right thing by staying together to raise the child. Whether they did the right thing by calling it Number Sixteen Bus Shelter is another question.

A judge in New Plymouth has just answered such a question. He has presided over the case of a girl called Tallulah Does the Hula from Hawaii and decreed that her name is, and I quote, 'an unnecessary social disability'.

The story has aroused a lot of interest because it is funny.

Yet the phrase Tallulah Does the Hula from Hawaii is no more than mildly amusing. It becomes a joke only when used as a name. And like most jokes it's only funny once. To the girl who got saddled with it, the joke wore off a long time ago. I'm not surprised she wanted to change it and I admire the judge for letting her.

Tallulah's parents remind me of a fat Australian I once saw in the Christchurch Botanic Gardens. He was wearing a yellow T-shirt that said, 'There are only two states to be in: Queensland or Pissed'. I thought it was funny.

Obviously the fat Australian thought it was funny too, which is why he wore the joke on his chest. But did he still find it funny after a month? As he stretched it over his gut for the fifteenth time did he still roar with laughter at the neatness of it? If so, he has the intellectual stature of a turnip. For the first and indispensable quality of a joke is surprise. A surprise repeated is a surprise no longer.

I presume fatso wore the T-shirt as a badge. He thought it said, 'Hey, I'm a funny person.' Actually it said, 'Hey, I'm so unfunny I have to wear jokes made up by someone else.' But at least he chose to wear the shirt himself.

Tallulah Does the Hula and Number Sixteen Bus Shelter did not get that choice. Their parents glued a T-shirt onto each of them at birth, obliging them to go forth and repeat the same joke for ever. It was a cruel thing to do.

And yet, for all their myopic cruelty, I think the parents of Tallulah and young master Number had a point. The names we give children are so few and dreary.

How many Johns are there in the world? The first message of being called John is conformity. Don't get above your station, sonny boy, you're no better than anyone else. And I can't help feeling that the names we give children influence the way they grow up. How else to explain that I've never met a Sid who sparkled or a Joy who didn't? Or a Rupert who wasn't Rupertish.

There are two problems with finding a unique name for a child. One is that babies give few clues to their eventual characters. If we were all christened according to our early natures the world would be awash with adults called Incontinent or Crumpleface.

The second problem is that there are people out there who have voted at some time in their lives for New Zealand First. And it's statistically probable that some of them will have worked out how to breed. What sort of names are they going to come up with?

American Indians solved the problem, I believe, by naming their children after the first thing Mother saw post partum. That's all very well in a wigwam where you're surrounded by natural abundance but these days it would lead to kids called Oxygen Mask or Fainting Husband or Midwife with Face of Boot.

So I suppose, reluctantly, that the kindest thing is to carry on calling them John or Mary and just hope they find a way of being themselves.

Recalling the grizzly

I am not a cognitive neuro-scientist but I recently met one at a party. He told me rather a lot about memory. I've forgotten most of it, of course, but I do recall him telling me that memory comes in long-term and short-term varieties and that neither is much cop. The short-term memory's feeble; the long-term memory's fictional.

Every second of every day we are besieged by trillions of bits of sensory data. Most of it simply bypasses the memory banks and heads straight for the great sea of oblivion. If it didn't our heads would soon bulge out to one side and then burst.

Apparently the short-term memory, even when in mid-season form, can only hang on to about half a dozen separate bits of stuff. Permanently excluded from that half dozen are the name of the person you've just been introduced to and where you put your glasses. But at least the short-term memory is honest. What little it hangs on to is by and large true.

The long-term memory is a lot more capacious but a lot less honest. It works like a Marxist historian. It revises the past.

Imagine you lived in Alaska and were attacked, as happens frequently in those parts, by a grizzly bear. Your response would be threefold. First you would fight to survive. The correct way to do so, apparently, is not to run, scream, sing a hymn or kick the bear in the crotch. That sort of carry-on only keeps the bear interested, especially the hymn-singing. The thing to do is to lie very still and wait for the bear to get bored and go away. I'm not sure I could manage that but it comes naturally to Alaskans, thereby allowing them to move on to the second stage of the process, which is to go to hospital for repairs. The third and final stage is to go to a party to tell people about your battle with a bear.

Because the event was traumatic your memory will have retained a vivid and reasonably accurate record of it. So you corner your victim between the fridge and the stove and tell him about it. Halfway through your riveting life-and-death narrative he glances over your shoulder, pretends to catch sight of someone he knows, promises to be back in seconds and you never see him again.

You now have two choices. Either you accept that your grizzly encounter was nothing startling on the Alaskan cocktail circuit, or you resolve to tell it better. In order to tell it better you heighten the good bits and expunge the dull bits. You turn it, in other words, into a story. And at the same time you turn it into a new memory. Because according to Mr Neuro, and who am I to argue with science, though I did for a bit out of habit, the long-term memory resembles a computer program that keeps receiving updates from Microsoft Central. Every time you tell a story the memory erases what actually happened and replaces it with your latest version of what happened. Eventually there's none of the original program left and the truth and your story have had a divorce.

Mr Neuro also told me that the memory, in common

with most of us, doesn't like nasty things. So it tends to discard them or soften them. We can remember for example the fact of feeling pain but we can't remember the actual sensation of pain.

All of which seems to me to explain rather a lot. It explains why mothers are prepared to have a second child. It explained why Messrs Glenn and Peters can tell conflicting versions of the same event and both believe they're telling the truth (though I'll wager a pig to a peanut that one's far closer to the truth than the other). It explains why people keep buying new pieces of exercise equipment. It explains why the sun always shone when you were a kid. It explains the enormous importance we attach to stories. It even explains why people continue to travel. 'Travel,' said Paul Theroux, and he's done a fair bit of it, 'is only glamorous in retrospect.' But retrospect is all we've got and it tells fibs. So we sit on our suitcases to close them once more and head off to the airport like innocents.

And it explains nostalgia. Today is just a welter of sensory data that is neither satisfactory nor coherent. But 20 years from now September 2008 will be the wonderland of yesterday when the weather was perfect, kids knew discipline, people knew their neighbours, everyone pulled together, the All Blacks were invincible and petrol was so cheap they effectively gave it away.

'The past is a foreign country,' wrote L.P. Hartley, 'they do things differently there.' It isn't. They don't. We've merely rewritten it in our heads.

Whale problems

There was a cracking bit of porn in the paper this morning. Like most porn it was a photograph. We are visual beasts and photos go straight to the primitive bits of the brain, bypassing any ganglions that do critical analysis or other hard stuff.

The photo starred a killer whale. Killer whales have become orcas in recent years in order to improve their chances of attracting funding. But killer isn't a bad name for them. They're the world's biggest carnivores. They do a lot of killing. And the one in the photo is trying to do a bit more. Its target is a baby sea lion with adorable eyelashes.

The sea lion is frolicking in the surf as youngsters do, having fun and texting its mates. Then up through the surf erupts the killer whale. It is roughly the size of Stewart Island and it's peckish. Judging by the relative positions of the two beasts I reckon it's 50/50 whether the sea lion will have made it to puberty.

The photo elicits two immediate Disneyesque responses. The first is, 'Run, baby sea lion, run, or the monster will eat you.' This is not helpful. Sea lions aren't built to run. They've got flippers rather than legs. Nevertheless if the little diddums managed to haul itself and its eyelashes a few metres up the sand it may have just escaped the plunging leviathan. If it panicked and headed for the sea, then it became a snack.

Sea lions generally hang around in packs so what this one was doing all alone on the beach is not clear. I suspect it had been placed there as bait, in which case one hopes the killer whale made a last-minute change of direction and got the pornographer. But the fact that the picture's in the paper suggests otherwise.

The second Disneyesque response is a desire to biff the whale on the nose and to tell it firmly to go and pick on something its own size. Oddly enough the whale would agree with you.

When you're the size of Stewart Island it's hard work flinging yourself onto a beach for what is little more than a morsel. What orcas far prefer to chow down on is a whale. They are especially fond of sperm whales, which don't sound all that appetising to me, but it takes all sorts.

Which brings us to the nub of the matter, and the ostensible reason for printing this porn in a family newspaper. There just aren't enough sperm whales around to keep killer whales fed. So killer whales are increasingly obliged to eat diddumsy sea lion pups and other marine mammals. And the terrible consequence is that sea otters, several brands of seal and the Steller's sea lion are now in danger of extinction.

But the problem actually goes back way beyond killer whales. The prime reason that the seals, otters and sea lions are low in numbers is not killer whales but us. In the 19th century we hunted these mammals close to extinction. Their populations have never recovered. And we are also the reason there aren't enough sperm whales for the killer whales to eat. We turned them into corsets and lamp oil in such enormous numbers that a killer whale now has to travel an awfully long way to find its habitual lunch. Hence its growing need to snack on creatures that we find endearing.

All of which presents a terrible dilemma for David Attenborough types. If they want to preserve the sea otter and its furry mates they're going to have to cull a substantial number of killer whales. And that seems like robbing Peter to pay Paul, especially when they've expended millions of hard-begged dollars over the last couple of decades rebranding killer whales as orcas and teaching us to love them.

There is, however, another solution to the problem that no one has suggested yet, but which is far more in accord with natural justice. The point is that you and I are responsible for this mess so it's only fair that we should suffer to clean it up. In other words, there needs to be a scientific cull of human beings. We could start by tossing wildlife pornographers to the orcas , but that would barely dent the problem. We need to get rid of several billion people if we're going to make a difference, and I somehow doubt that there's the political will to do that at the squidgy-hearted UN.

Not to worry, though. Time and natural forces will sort everything out in the end. Give it 100 years or so and I think matters will have resolved themselves, one way or the other. And my bet's on the other.

The liturgy remains

Things change, and it is the duty of crusty old men to bemoan change. Take rugby.

I used to play rugby and I understood the rules. The main rule was to avoid fights, large opponents and, as far as possible, the ball. The older I got the better I became at obeying this rule and I found rugby an increasingly pleasant way to pass a Saturday afternoon. And it led to an even more pleasant Saturday evening that had a habit of stretching into Sunday.

Last weekend I watched a Super 14 game on television, thereby doubling the ratings. I found that I no longer understood the sport. I didn't understand why it was called super, I didn't understand why the other viewer was still watching, I didn't understand why the referee kept shouting and I didn't understand the rules. Nor, it seemed, did the players, which is perhaps why the referee kept shouting. But I did understand why there were so few people on the terraces. It was because the game consisted mainly of penalties and scrums.

Scrums have changed. The modern scrum requires the ref to act like the caller at a barn dance. 'Crouch and touch, nicely now, and pause and, oh dear, we seem to have fallen over. Let's try that again, shall we?'

At one point the ref summoned the captains like a headmaster calling schoolboys to his study, and insisted that, come what may and in despite of the players' efforts to thwart him, he was going to 'free this game up'. He did this by banishing players from the field for dastardly crimes like neglecting to roll or not going through an imaginary gate, crimes that neither I nor they understood. If he'd persisted and reduced each team to three players he might have freed the game up. But he didn't. When I awoke there was motor racing on the television. It seemed almost interesting.

Nevertheless I'm delighted to say that although the rules of rugby have changed to an extent that has rendered the national game almost unrecognisable, some things have remained as fixed as the stars in the sky. And one of those things is the commentary. So, with a nod of acknowledgement to Flann O'Brien, who invented this device, here's a little catechism of cliché to test your grasp of the commentator's ageless art.

What meteorological phenomenon has the habit of accompanying an injury?

A cloud.

In relation to an injury cloud, where is the player invariably situated?

Under it.

If two players have a minor altercation, in which two verbs are they said to indulge?

Push and shove.

A lot of push and shove?

No, a bit of push and shove.

What is the difference between push and shove?

Next question, please.

If the bit of push and shove rises in intensity but still falls short of the sort of uninhibited fist fight that would bring the crowds back to rugby, what female fashion accessories are the players remarkably and inexplicably said to make use of?

Handbags.

If, as a result of push, shove or handbags, there occurs a breach of the skin in one or other of the combatants, to what quaintly old-fashioned oenological product is the consequent exudation of bodily fluid compared?

Can you repeat that?

No.

Claret.

Well done. From which region of France does claret come?

I thought this quiz was about rugby.

Very well, but give yourself a mark for Bordeaux. If a player inadvertently loses the ball when pressured by opponents, what expectorant function is he said to employ?

He coughs the ball.

May he cough the ball in the direction of his choice?

No. Only up.

What undefined but visually disabling artefact is a prominent player said to be having?

A blinder.

And if a player displays an exceptional propensity for swift movement, of what insignificant body part is he said to display an impressive quantity?

Toe.

Could this perhaps be tow?

It would make as much sense.

What ruse of gambling is used to describe the suddenly increased efforts of a team?

The ante.

Does the team raise the ante?

No, it ups it.

In what way can the raising of stakes prior to receiving cards in a game of poker be considered comparable to the increased efforts of a team to win a rugby game?

Search me.

To what outmoded domestic implement is the centre of a player's body compared?

The bread basket.

In what direction can you not put with any more of this?

Up.

Good.

Water works

There are lots of religions but only two possibilities. Possibility One is that all religions have got it wrong. Possibility Two is that one of them has got it right and the rest have got it wrong.

Whichever possibility is correct — and one of them has to be — the inescapable conclusion is that over the millennia there have been billions of wasted Sunday mornings, silly uniforms worn without reason, lies printed and sold as the truth, heretics unjustifiably burned, countries wrongly invaded and goats sacrificed to no effect. I feel upset about the goats. Goats subscribe to Possibility One, so it seems unfair that they should have been dragged onto altars they didn't believe in to have their throats slit.

The goats, however, are wrong. The answer to the Riddle of the Two Possibilities is Possibility Two. One religion is right, the rest wrong. The right one is Buddhism.

But not Buddhism as practised by temple-going worshippers. Most of Buddhism, like all the other faiths, is accreted ritualistic bunkum. Some 25 centuries ago, however, old Budds got one thing right. That thing was reincarnation. Sort of.

Every one of us and every bit of every one of us has been multiply recycled. It is a statistical certainty that your body houses a bit of Julius Caesar. And of Dr Crippen. And of Elvis. And of a compacted star. If you don't believe me, just go and find someone sciency to show you the maths, then come back and apologise.

There is a finite amount of matter in the world. It's like a tub of plasticine. It can and does get formed into an effectively infinite number of shapes. Bits of you have previously been bits of stegosauri and rabbits and krill and broccoli. And will be again, except for the stegosauri. Buddha knew his science before science did.

It's an easy and comforting step from there to the hope that after you've died your personal chunk of atoms will choose to stick together and become something else en masse. They won't. They'll just scatter. But it's a nice thought. And with it comes the notion of what you'd like to come back as next time. Well, I want to come back as a plumber.

The flush toilet is a fine thing. Every day it permits us to send a few trillion trillion atoms away on their journey to become broccoli or krill and to pretend it hasn't happened. But a blocked toilet is a grim thing. On flushing, the waters swirl and rise towards the rim and we look on in impotent horror. We are threatened with a flood of digestive truth.

I just underwent such a threat. The waters settled eventually millimetres from the rim. Whereupon I went off in search of my miracle tool, the long-handled plunger. I love its dome of sturdy flexibility. I love its belch-making simplicity. I love it so much I could kiss it, almost.

I plunged. Gurgles and burps and sumptuous sucking noises and an eruption of cigarette ends and the water with its grim freight simply swirled and sank to the level of obedience. It was just so satisfying. Working with water always is.

Mike is my age, but he has a four-year-old daughter.

Yesterday he came in with joy in his eye and told me of a game he'd been playing with her. They'd been throwing bits of grass and wood into a culvert and then rushing across the road to watch them emerge the other side.

'Pooh sticks,' I said, 'you were playing Pooh sticks. You know, Winnie-the-Pooh.' He'd never read Winnie-the-Pooh. He'd just rediscovered the joy of water.

Rain has inundated these parts for months. Hill tracks have become streams. Until walked, that is, by me and my pup. The pup has stood for hours as I have diverted stream after stream, digging ditches with my gumboot, shaping the flow, judging the inexorable effects of gravity, creating miniature reservoirs and islands and deltas and dams. I've drowned land. I've reclaimed land. I've been engrossed, involved. The dog has been puzzled. Why weren't we moving forward to hunt in answer to a dog's incessant urge. 'Be patient,' I'd say, 'bits of me have been dog, but all of me is now human, so I am working with water. I find it good in a way you can't grasp.'

When we've taken the same track some days later, time and again I have found that other human organisms have modified my dykes and dams and culverts, added a tributary stream or a holding pond or a weir of pebbles.

Where does it come from, this delight in working with water? I cannot tell you. Perhaps it's some dim acknowledgement of the inevitable spiral of all the world's constituents back to the sea that bore them.

'If I were called in to construct a religion,' wrote Larkin, 'I should make use of water.' Me too.

Tip it in

Tip it in. Go on, by the fistful. Into the daily bread. Give us this day our folic acid. And why stop there? Let's fill our bread with everything that does good. Let's eat our way to an untroubled life, unfailing happiness and unlimited sex. Put a boffin in every bakery and all manner of things shall be well.

It's a rum old world so let's de-rum it. I want the recipe for bread to read like a pharmaceutical catalogue. We're all just a heap of chemicals, so let's manipulate the heap a bit. It ought to be easy.

Consider blonde hair and big breasts. Yes, yes, I know, but I'm not here to be nice. I'm here to tell the truth. The truth is that lots of women, and I do not pass judgement on them, want blonde hair and big breasts. The hair dye and implant statistics tell us this, as does a glance at any female presenter on Fox television, or any festival of country and western music.

Lots of men, and I do not pass judgement on them either, also want women to have blonde hair and big breasts. They want to go to bed with such women. Which is presumably why lots of women go to great lengths and expense to acquire these things. The women may not want to go to bed with the men, but they like the sensation of men wanting to go to bed with them. All of which adds fizz to a flat world.

So how wonderful if Dr Test-tube were to isolate the bits

of chemical programming that bleach the hair and swell the chest and then biff them into every sliced white sandwich loaf. It would save a lot of expense and medical peril and it would make millions of people happy and we'd all look Swedish. Though, as it happens, the Swedish aren't that happy. Indeed they come near the top of the league tables for gloom.

No matter. We can solve misery with bread as well. And we've already got what we need. All that's required is to load the trucks with Prozac and Valium and send sackfuls of each to every bakery in the land. We could waste a lot of time debating which of the two is preferable, but the elegant solution is to use both.

'But Valium and Prozac are addictive,' squeals Dr Worrypot. 'Once hooked, people have enormous trouble unhooking themselves.'

To which, my dear Dr Worrypot, I can only reply that you could say the same thing about oxygen. We're all inescapably addicted to it yet no one seems to fret about it. And if we follow my recipe for bread and joy then we won't have to fret about anything. Peace of mind will become as freely and constantly available as the air we breathe. And no one will need to unhook. They'll just fix themselves a sandwich and get themselves a fix. Easy, see? The result is that we'll all stop worrying, and what is there to worry about in stopping worrying? As any doc will tell you, worry kills. There's too much of it about. So let's bop it on the head with bread.

And let's bop lots of other stuff on the head at the same time. The possibilities are limitless. A squirt of Tamiflu into every cheese vienna and we can sneer at swine flu, bird flu and all the future flus that we're bound to be threatened with in the increasingly terrified years ahead, as the end of the world as we know it looms like a Hammer Horror jelly monster. With guaranteed national immunity we can become the tourist destination of choice for the rich and frightened. They'll clamour for our company and our bread. And once here they'll find that we are all so Prozac-peaceable that they'll want to stay and snuggle up to our great big breasts.

We'll become the idyllic ukulele-strumming, stress-free island in the South Pacific that Gauguin thought he'd found and kept painting pictures of until he went down in a screaming pus-laden heap as a result of having contracted syphilis. But our visitors won't contract syphilis. Penicillin in the bagels will see to that. And the tourists will be so very grateful that they'll toss cash around like confetti and encourage their neighbours to come join them down here in the lifelong singalong of happiness, and we won't have to work any more because the cash just keeps flooding in from overseas and we won't feel guilty about it because of all our lovely bread and we'll just lounge around being beautiful, blond and wealthy and while the rest of the world chokes on its own growth and pollution we'll just strum our ukuleles. Bliss. And all for the price of a loaf of bread. Tip it in, I say.

Go away and leave me alone

Iceland is apparently in danger of insolvency. It has binged on debt. It has behaved like an obese American shopper in one of those flannelette romper suits that look just about OK on babies, but terminally saddening on adults. Iceland has borrowed heaps of dosh from the world's dosh-palaces, and now, with fear stalking their vaults, the dosh-palaces want it back. Iceland can't pay, can't borrow from anyone else because there isn't anyone else, and may go under. Which will be bad news for walruses.

The Icelandic middle classes will have to forsake their newly acquired habits of global excellence — scuba holidays in the Maldives, wine-tasting classes, magnetic mattresses, frappaccinos, gym membership and overnight bags with little wheels — and go back to igloos and subsistence farming. Subsistence farming in Iceland means sitting by a hole in the ice with a club and waiting for a walrus to surface, whereupon whammo, the walrus becomes the lender of last resort, handing over its meat for food, its blubber for fuel, its whiskers for fishing line and its tusks for something to whittle in the 24-hour nights that afflict those parts for half the year.

Now, if Iceland slides into the cold ocean of bankruptcy, can we be far behind? We're about the same size as Iceland and similarly in debt. What's worse, we haven't got walruses. Nor do we any longer have the easy-beat moa, one of whose drumsticks would feed a family of four with something left over for the dog. If we go under we'll be reduced to hunting and eating stoats. But at least I won't get any more letters from Meridian.

'Dear Mr Bennett,' it began, which was frankly astonishing. In the light of the rest of the 'letter' a more apt opening line would have been 'Dear Diddums'. Because Meridian chose to address me, an autonomous 51-year-old adult, as if I were six.

'We asked our accounts team to look at your usage and challenged them to see if anything needs changing . . . Our bean counters got their abacuses out and sharpened their pencils. Based on their calculations . . . it seems you're already on the right plan to suit your usage.'

Where do I begin with this tripe? Well, I would like to begin with the slab-faced 'executive' who sanctioned it. I'd like to cram his pallid corrugated flesh into an XXOS perambulator and wheel him through the streets inviting Meridian customers to lean halitotically over him saying, 'Who's a bonnie wee boy then?', seizing his jowls between thumb and forefinger to give them a good painful tug, planting bristly kisses on the burst blood vessels of his cheeks, wondering in a high-pitched voice whether he's had a little accident and jabbing his shrivelled genitalia with nappy pins till he expires from humiliation.

Meridian sells electricity. I buy it. Our relationship is commercial. I don't care about them and they don't care about me. I know that. They know that. But they pretend otherwise. And they expect me to fall for it. They expect me to believe that they look out for my interests, that they instruct their — do they have to? — 'bean counters' to check that I'm getting the best possible deal, using their — oh my God and pass the gin — abacuses. It's about as humorous as tetraplegia and it's all lies. Obvious, demeaning, patronising lies.

'Plus,' they continue, 'have you heard about My Meridian?'

My Meridian? My bloody Meridian! Like My Little Pony. Or My First Bicycle. Or the infantilising My Documents folder that comes with My Computer Software and that infuriates me every time it appears on screen yet seems impossible to erase.

'It's a cool web tool for getting your bills delivered online . . . To have a play just go to . . .'

No. I am not going to 'have a play', however 'cool' your 'tool' may be. Look. I know that a recent survey revealed that 45 per cent of so-called adults play computer games daily, but that still leaves a slim majority of us who choose to make some effort at being grown-ups, who do not demand constant entertaining and who strive to see the world as it is rather than dwelling in a fantasy land of computer-generated bloodbaths or Disney fibs or lifestyle choices or Oprah Bloody Winfrey or low-fat gyms or positive thinking or fundamentalist religion or five-plus-a-day or Lotto or advertising lala-land or any of the other infantilising tosh that is spewed out to generate money by encouraging us to remain in nappies.

For Meridian is not alone. The defining quality of 21st-century western consumption is an increasing reluctance to grow up, a reluctance that is fostered by commerce and media and government for the simple reason that babies are easier to manipulate.

And though I don't fancy a financial implosion and the consequent poverty, there are moments when it seems preferable to the tsunami of infantile tosh that I am subjected to daily. Pass the stoat.

Ida down

She didn't know it, but her name was Ida. Ida was rapacious. And she knew that others were rapacious too. So when she went to the lake to drink one morning she did so warily. Predators could lurk. She stood still, sniffed the air, detected no threats to her well-being and cautiously lowered her muzzle to drink.

As she did so she breathed in and felt woozy. For just above the water there hovered a pall of marsh gas. She breathed in again, felt woozier, wondered briefly what was going on, what unseen enemy had seized her, then she lost consciousness. She crumpled, and slid down the damp bank. The water accepted her as water does. The ripples spread, then the surface calmed to a mirror. Ida was gone.

She sank slowly, turning as she sank, and came to rest on the soft lakebed. Mud settled around her. It entombed her. Slowly, slowly the mud became rock. And so did Ida.

Ida had left offspring. They noted her absence but at least one of them got over it without counselling, and went on to have offspring of her own. And those offspring had offspring. And those . . . But perhaps we had better fast forward a little. We'll fast forward 47 million years.

They were eventful years. Over the course of them one line of Ida's descendants learned to walk upright, shed their tails, lost most of their fur, invented agriculture, invented money, invented writing, invented God (who looked remarkably like the inventor), invented the soul (though denying one to their multiply-great Grandma Ida), invented a sophisticated range of weapons with which to kill each other and thus exercise their rapacity, then finally, and most impressively of all, invented democracy. The aim of democracy was to curb rapacity.

Let's zoom in on one of those descendants. He's a democrat through and through. So committed a democrat, indeed, that he has been elected to that mother of all democracies, the British House of Commons.

Zoom in more closely and we will see that he is filling in a claim for expenses incurred while performing his democratic duties. 'Item,' he writes, 'one floating ornamental island for duckpond: £4000.' He staples the receipt to the form, sniffs the air, detects no threat to his well-being and submits the claim.

A few weeks later, in the mother of all democracies, there is the mother of all rows. Some snitch of a journalist has obtained the expense claims of MPs. The ornamental island has been hauled from its duckpond and dumped on the front page, alongside £2000 mirrors, interest payments on non-existent mortgages, and the bill for dredging an MP's private moat.

The resultant eruption of shock and outrage is so violent that it reaches these distant islands. How did you feel when you heard the news? Were you shocked? Were you outraged? No, nor was I. I enjoyed every bit of it. I longed for the journos to uncover ever more flagrant abuses. I wanted the MPs to have claimed for liposuction or polo ponies or massages of a non-therapeutic nature.

Partly this was just the pleasure of seeing one's betters

with their trousers down. And part of that pleasure was the confirmation that my betters are no better than I am. For if I were in a position to fiddle expenses, I'd probably fiddle them. You wouldn't, I'm sure, but I would. At several schools where I taught, stationery was available on an honesty system. I knew the system but lacked the honesty. I filled my house with pens and paper. The difference between me and the MPs is one of scale and opportunity only. We are all descendants of Ida.

So I was not surprised by the news. And nor would most of the world have been. Indeed most of the world would have been astonished that anyone felt surprise. For most of the world is corrupt. Try getting anywhere in the Philippines without bribing. Or in Italy. And both these places are nominal democracies. As is South Korea, where a former prime minister, accused of taking bribes, has just tossed himself off a cliff. Human history is the story of the abuse of power.

A just democracy is as rare as missing link fossils. Those of us who live under one are blessed. Thanks to democracy I've gone 50 years without once being assaulted, and I've been robbed only by power companies. In other words, I've had an easier time of it than any of Ida's 47 million years' worth of descendants. And if the entertaining expenses row reminds us how lucky we are and that the price of freedom is constant vigilance, then it will have been a good thing.

As for the fossilised Ida, that priceless addition to our knowledge of our origins, well, the bloke who dug her up kept her to himself for years. Then he sold her for a million rapacious bucks. Ida would have understood that.

The day before Christmas

'Tis the day before Christmas and what could be worse
Than having a columnist break into verse?
But rhyme is the way that I want to relate
Some thoughts at the end of two thousand and eight.

'Tis the day before Christmas and all through the mall
The shoppers are purchasing nothing at all,
Having realised at last, although no one has said it,
That only a fool can be happy on credit.

The skulls of the shoppers now harbour a guest
Whom they didn't invite, but who's making a nest
And who's looking like staying on into next year
To bugger up everything. His name is Fear.

Fear that prosperity's over at last,
Fear that we're hurtling back to the past,
Fear that the thirties are coming again;
It isn't *if* poverty gets us, but *when*.

Thousands of people are heading to Oz,
Not for the weather but merely because
The grass will be green if they simply get out.
(Don't mention that Oz has got terminal drought.)

Up north in Alaska the temperature's getting
So frightfully high that the bears are all sweating,
The ice floes are melting, the mooses are wailing
(Unless they've already been shot by Ms Palin).

Ms Palin's a born-again Christian who knows
That everything's good because God made it so,
But saying that God's in his heaven can hardly
Explain the existence of Robert Mugabe,
And if there's a God, how come in Iraq
A journalist's sandal flew wide of its mark?

I'm sorry I don't know the shoe-thrower's name
But I do know his only mistake was his aim.
If he'd taken a little more care when he hurled,
He could have brought limitless joy to the world.

I'm sure all the same there is much to relate
That did produce joy in two thousand and eight
But as we're approaching the end of December
I'm finding it awfully hard to remember.

So just at the moment that students in Greece
Are out on the streets biffing rocks at police
Intent on reducing to rubble and strife
The land that gave birth to our whole way of life,
And we're once more reminded, this holiday season,
The dominant force in this world isn't reason.
But rather a cocktail of fear and desire
That makes us leap straight from the pan to the fire,
I find myself sitting here scratching my pate
In a bid to remember two thousand and eight.

Ah yes, in November we went to the polls
And, just as we knew it would, Labour got rolled,
But all I recall of that epochal night
Was how it resembled a primitive rite.

For much as the ancients would offer a virgin
To try and ensure that their paddocks would burgeon,
So we all endeavoured to foster the crop
By building a bonfire with Helen on top.
It wasn't as though she'd done anything wrong,
She'd simply been king of the castle too long.

Some weeks before Christmas a fellow called Ritchie
Split up with Madonna and got very rich. He'll
Be pleased with the money but must wonder how
He ever got hitched to that terrible cow.
She's fifty years old and she's not worth a whistle
(Even Ritchie himself has compared her to gristle)
But the point of Madonna, the ludicrous truth,
Is her quest for the grail of perpetual youth.
(The same stunt was tried by a Dorian Gray
And he ended up in a horrible way.)
All her fame and her wealth and her mansions are built on
The same sort of sand that lies under Miss Hilton.

So perhaps as we come to the end of the year
I've struck on a reason to bring out the beer:
In two thousand and nine as economies crumble
And bankers run naked and stock markets tumble
And Chrysler and Ford and General Motors
Acknowledge their cars aren't as good as Toyota's

And God takes a look at the chaos and snickers
Thus sending the chill wind of fear up our knickers
Perhaps we'll lose interest in Paris and Britney
And other celebs of a similar kidney.

(I'm sorry to end on a terrible rhyme
But it's late and I've opened a bottle of wine
And I'm raising a glass of 6.99 red
To you and my dog. Then I'm going to bed.)

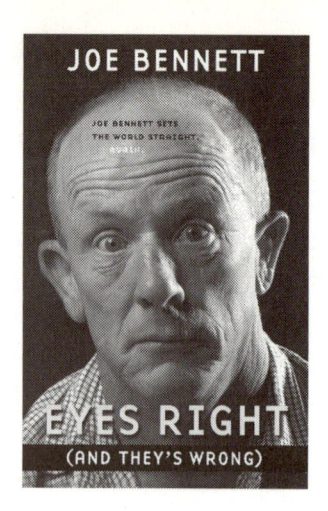

Eyes Right (and They's Wrong)
Joe Bennett

In the last year New Zealand's favourite columnist has turned fifty, lost a dog, been to China, been motivationally spoken to, built a goatshed, drunk with a Bangkok Buddhist, survived Christmas, eavesdropped Winnie with Condoleezza and . . . but why not let him tell you about it himself? *Eyes Right (and They's Wrong)* is Joe Bennett at his ruthless, funniest best. There's no more to say, really.

He continues to live in Lyttelton. Just.

HarperCollins*Publishers*

Laugh? I Could Have Cried
Joe Bennett

Joe Bennett was born into the middle classes of England in 1957. Life was stable, suburban and sunny. Computers weren't around to ruin his childhood, nor terror of paedophiles, nor fast food. He had it easy.

Aged 29, he came to New Zealand for one year to teach. Aged 51, he's still here. But in 1998 he swapped the classroom for the opinion page of the nation's newspapers. Since then, Joe Bennett has been Qantas Media Awards Columnist of the Year three times, he's had eleven collections of his columns published in New Zealand and three worldwide, he's written three best-selling travel books, he's become a regular on radio and television, and he has made far too many after-dinner speeches.

Laugh? I Could Have Cried presents the very best of a decade's work, organized by topic. Here are his most memorable thoughts on dogs, games, language, travel, the idiocy of belief, and the swamping trivia that shape our lives despite our best intentions, all of them written with the ferocious comic clarity that has made his name.

HarperCollins*Publishers*

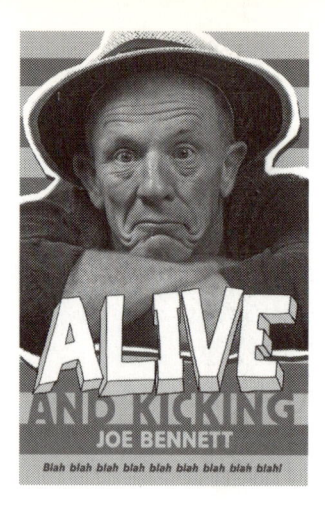

Alive and Kicking
Joe Bennett

Still alive after 11 years and 11 collections of columns, Joe Bennett sticks the boot into Beckhamania, golf umbrellas, beer ads, Hillary Clinton, all sorts of bureaucrats, and a fatso from the Middle East who flies halfway round the world to shoot our deer. But he writes loving stuff, too, about fish and postcards and Pavarotti and butter and dead dogs.

From his fastness in Lyttelton, New Zealand's best-loved columnist once again dissects the weird, wide and sometimes less than wonderful world with peerless wit and concision.

HarperCollins*Publishers*